To Peggy:

Hope you enjoy the
Drive-Thru!.

-Thank you for your order!

Mike W. LG

"The Drive-Thru is the easy choice made by many. Few are brave enough to make the best choice, to go in, place the order, and leave more efficiently. Mike takes on this topic and motivates the reader to explore new and different ways of looking at life experiences."

—Tom Ziglar, CEO of Zig Ziglar Corporation, Speaker, and Author

"Mike translates his life and public-speaking experiences into common sense life lessons."

—Jeffrey J. Fox, best-selling author of *How to Become a Rainmaker* and twelve other international best sellers

"Success isn't a one size fits all, but with Mike's leadership, reaching new heights is possible for everyone. This book shares smart, short stories, each with a key takeaway to improve our everyday lives."

—Shannon Kaiser, best-selling author of *The Self-Love Experiment* and *Joy Seeker*

"Mike shares his experiences in such a way that we are able to relate to his lessons and walk away with the inspiration to focus on those opportunities that are most important to us."

—Peggy Libbey, CEO of Redwood Collaborative Media and Software Test Professionals Conference

"Mike shares his passion to help each of us learn new ways to accomplish our mission and goals in life by showing us creative approaches and alternatives to reaching success"

—John Miles, Partner, Virgo Investment Group
and Founder of Ovesto Capital

"Through incredible, true life experiences, Mike inspires his readers to grow both personally and professionally."

—Amberly Lago, best-selling author of *True Grit and Grace*

"Mike has creatively assembled over 20 years of experience, coaching, and leadership into a motivating and inspiring masterpiece. This book will help readers reclaim their Best Self on the journey of life!"

—Dr. Chasity K. Adams, Licensed Psychologist, Author
of Reclaiming Your Best Self, Speaker & Life Coach

"Love this book! In a world where the fast eat the slow, the convenience of the drive-thru doesn't always meet one's needs. This book helps us think differently, using great stories to drive the points home."

—Jason Jennings, NY Times, WSJ and USA TODAY best-
selling author of eight books including, The Reinventors.

The Drive-Thru Is NOT Always Faster

—— MIKE W LYLES ——

Mike Lyles Consulting, LLC.

2019

First Printing: 2019

ISBN 978-0-57821-980-6 (Paperback)
ISBN 978-1-54398-702-7 (E-Book)

Mike Lyles Consulting, LLC
125 Foxglove Drive
Statesville, NC 28625

www.MikeWLyles.com

Ordering Information:

Special discounts are available on quantity purchases by corporations, associations, educators, and others. For details, contact the publisher at the above listed address.

US trade bookstores and wholesalers: Please contact:
Mike Lyles Consulting, LLC
Telephone: (336) 468-7336 or email info@mikewlyles.com

This book is dedicated to my mom, Jenny Lyles. Thanks, Mom, for being the first "motivational speaker" to ever impact my life.

Contents

Acknowledgments

My life has prepared me for the things I have shared in this book. I have been blessed to meet so many great people who have influenced the decisions I made and the stories I will tell you in the pages that follow.

I would like to thank so many people who contributed to making this book a reality.

My mom, Jenny Lyles, was my first teacher. She taught me humility. She taught me that you can care for others even when they treat you wrongly or don't respect you back. I watched her bravely stand in front of crowds, large and small, and inspire them with her words. The most amazing thing I want each of you to take away from this is that she didn't even realize the impact she was making. You never know who is watching your life. You never know when something you are doing could change someone's life forever. For my first book, I want to give a special thanks to my mom, the first person who had faith in me throughout all of my life.

I would also like to thank each and every person that never failed to ask, "When is your book coming out?" You will never know how much it inspired, motivated, and helped me to keep pressing forward.

A special thanks to Greg Collins for creating my book cover and my book website. Thanks to my book coach and bestselling author, Shannon Kaiser, and to my editor, Brianne Bardusch, for supporting my final manuscript. Thanks to bestselling author and friend, Jeffrey Fox, for the valuable input and edits.

To those who gave support on the material, the content, and the wording in this book, I owe a great debt of gratitude. You know exactly who you are and how you impacted this book.

Foreword

A great book is a pleasure to read and offers a lesson that you can wrap your mind around. Experience is the best teacher if you learn from the lessons that come with your success and failures.

Mike has superior observation skills and is a good listener that examines challenges and opportunities from many angles, so his opinions are sound and well thought out. This book is no exception.

What you will find, in the chapters that follow, are many of life's lessons that, frankly, we can all learn something from and apply at different points in our lives.

Pay it forward, read the book, and then pass on the lessons when appropriate to friends and colleagues that could benefit from your personal coaching and Mike's writings.

A book like this can serve as a ready reference again and again.

Ron Blahnik
CIO & SVP
Strategy & Innovation, Supply Chain Logistics and Retail Analytics
Hibbett Sports

Introduction

In July 2002, I set down and started a diary of notes, leadership quotes, things I was learning, and suggestions for an upcoming book. Little did I know that it would be over a decade before I would sit down and pull it all together.

My first leadership mentor and I began working together in January 2002. By February 2002, I was making a list of everything I needed to accomplish and marking them off weekly.

A few months later, I purchased a book that would completely change my life. This book was *How to Become CEO* by Jeffrey J. Fox.

I began *officially* leading others in 1998. The feeling of accomplishment in helping people to reach their goals and achieve team and company goals was more than I imagined. I knew, even back then, that being a leader, mentor, and coach for others would be one of my core values.

In 2003, I became a manager, and the accomplishment of responsibility, ownership, and authority over expanding teams was amazing. I began reading books by great speakers and writers: Stephen Covey, Jeffrey Fox, John C. Maxwell, and Brian Tracy to name a few. I began to expand my leadership skills by taking pieces of information from these great speakers and others.

For years, I have compiled notes, experiences (good and bad), which I knew I would someday put into my first book. From the very start, I planned to call the book "Today is the first day of the *success* of your life." For years this was the title I planned to use. However, one day I was examining the old phrase "Today is the best day of the *rest* of your life." And I realized this phrase was correct; every day is the beginning of the rest of your life.

However, when I thought about "the *success*" of my life, I realized that many of the successful events in my life happened in the past. Throughout our life, if we give everything we have, we may have many opportunities to have those *success* moments. Keep your eyes open wide, look for those magical moments where you can gain even the smallest of successes along the way, and you will experience success over and over throughout your life.

Since the early years of following those initial speakers, I have been so blessed and honored to travel to five continents spanning multiple countries, meeting so many new people, speaking in front of thousands, and learning something new with every adventure. When I realized I was closing in on the final updates to my book, I set out to build a marketing program to sell my book, and to engage, interact, and connect with many people who speak, write, and follow motivational work. If I gave my list of those who have influenced and changed my ways of thinking, we would be stuck in this introduction for a long time. For each of you who have met me, shared your stories, written great books, created great podcasts and recordings, I thank you. I've made it a habit to meet those new writers in my space, and to buy their books in an effort to learn more in the world of motivational writing and talking. You will likely be able to distinguish those chapters I wrote in the early years versus those I wrote near the end. We all have the ability to grow, and I can honestly say I have grown so much since those first words written down for this book.

Through the years, I have enjoyed books that do not have to be read from chapter 1 until "The End." Each chapter is a separate short story. My book follows this same process. While each chapter is numbered, you will find you do not have to read them in order.

Thank you for taking the time to read my book. Without you, I would just be taking notes. You are now part of one of the many milestones in writing for me. I hope you enjoy it, and most of all, I hope you take something from it that you can use for yourself, as well as others who are part of your life.

Chapter 1:
Just Start It!

"If you don't have a mountain, build one and then
climb it. And after you climb it, build another one;
otherwise you start to flatline in your life."

Sylvester Stallone

In 1988, Nike launched "**Just Do It**" as a slogan that would become common-place. "Just Do It" means to get going, not be afraid to take that step, and be confident that you can accomplish anything you set out to complete.

Years ago, I was sitting in a meeting at work, planning the details of a project with my team. After a long meeting, someone interrupted with a statement that went something like this, "Just get started — we're wasting time."

In your life you should "Just Start It", which means get started, and do not allow yourself to be paralyzed by analysis and overthinking the plan. Jim Collins opens his book *Good to Great* with one powerful sentence that says, "Good is the enemy of great." We put off things today because we feel we don't have the time to do them perfectly. We delay getting started for days, weeks, months, and maybe even years. We keep waiting for that perfect opportunity or to have everything in place before we get started. But the truth is, we could simply just start now.

It's so easy to procrastinate. Many of us will complete dozens of things unrelated to the truly important work that needs to be done. Stephen Covey notes in *The 7 Habits of Highly Effective People* that you have to focus on what is *important* and less on what is *urgent*. We have to complete the *urgent + important*, but many times we focus on the things that are either *urgent + not important* or *not urgent + not important* and we fail to ever move to the true goals and aspirations for our lives.

Get started today. As you read this, you may be thinking of something you have always wanted to accomplish, complete, and give to the world. It could be one of many things. Most everyone has something they have wanted to accomplish. Don't let that dream sit on the shelf. Stop waiting for that perfect opportunity to align and get started on the little things that can move you step by step toward your ultimate goal. Start your journey now.

"Just Start It" may take some time to fully complete. For instance, if your goal is to be an airplane pilot, you obviously would not just jump on a plane, take the cockpit, and start flying. It would be disastrous. It would require you to take the training, learn the process, and then begin flying a plane. But even in this example, the first steps — taking the courses, getting instruction, learning the controls, educating yourself on aeronautics — are a simple way you can "Just Start It."

Get out there. Take those first steps. People will notice.

Just Start It! Be prepared to restart sometimes. Then keep going!

Chapter 2:
One Day

"Between stimulus and response there is a space. In that space lies our freedom and power to choose our response. In our response lies our growth and freedom."

Viktor E. Frankl, Man's Search for Meaning

One day you will wish you had spent time with your parents when they were younger and alive. You will think of hundreds of questions you should have asked them. And it will be too late to turn back time when you realize this.

One day you will regret the hours you spent at work doing little things that had nothing to do with your career or personal growth. Examine your contributions, determine if you are helping yourself or your company, and if you think you are not, then rebuild your game plan.

One day you will regret, if you're a parent, all the time you missed spending with your kids as they were growing up. The potential memories you can build with them will go with them for years and will very likely make them parents who share the same experiences with their children.

One day you will wonder why you procrastinated on your dreams and allowed other low priority tasks to keep you from doing at least one thing every day to move you further toward your ultimate goals. Don't let yourself focus on all of the lower priority things because they are easier to do. Don't ruin your opportunity to do something magical and important by allowing yourself to procrastinate.

One day you will recognize the impact you could have had on someone's life. Many people are looking for that one role model, that one example to follow. Don't let fear or lack of confidence hold you back from being the one who someone thinks of when they say, "They changed my life." Leave a legacy.

But I have good news for you . . .

- One day is all it takes to call that parent, have dinner with them, or give them a visit.

- One day is all it takes to assess your contributions to your company and your career.

- One day is all it takes to change the time you spend with your kids.

- One day is all it takes to document your dreams and begin working on them in priority.

- One day is all it takes to show someone you care and give them a helping hand.

One day you will realize that every day is a blessing.

Are there things you are neglecting in your life? Are you putting off something or neglecting an area in your life because you think you have all the time in the world to "do it later"? The past is gone. The future is not promised. We have today. This is the *one day* you can depend on.

One day, this will all make sense to you. Don't waste your time. I have always said, "Regret is the most expensive emotion." We hear stories every day of people who wish they had that "opportunity" one more time. Don't let this happen to you.

You still have time.

Chapter 3:
Make a Mountain Out of an Ant Hill

"Never give up on something that you can't
go a day without thinking about."

Sir Winston Churchill

There is an old phrase that says, "Don't make a mountain out of a mole hill." The phrase is intended to make us remember there are no setbacks in life that should become so large in our minds that we build them into something so large they make us want to give up.

I was walking through my yard, and I stumbled across a small pile of dirt. Without even thinking, I brushed my foot across it. To my surprise, I realized something I should have already known. This was an ant hill. And ants were scurrying in every direction, shocked by the demise of their "hill."

Then something occurred to me that changed my perception of this situation. Ants don't take time to worry about "What happened?" or "Why did this happen to me?" or "We must give up now; our hill has been destroyed." Instead, they immediately go back to work on building the hill back up, restoring the work they had done.

Most people do not operate this way. When we have a setback, we lean toward giving up. Someone at work doesn't like us, so we stop working hard. Our peers make fun of our goal, so we give it up. Our boss gives us constructive criticism, and it turns our work life so far upside down that we spend so much time replaying the situation in our mind and we can't concentrate on being the best at our job. Someone makes a joke about a goal we are trying to meet, and we feel too embarrassed to keep trying. Some emergency, accident, or health issue occurs in our lives, and we feel there is no way we can keep moving in the direction of our dreams.

Life is going to give you setbacks from time to time. Small disappointments will make you feel it's not worth adjusting or restarting. When this happens, you must focus on the big picture and the importance of what you're trying to accomplish.

As long as there are people around ant hills, there will be a risk of those hills being knocked down or destroyed. The same applies to each of us. The more people you are around, the greater the risk of someone affecting your hard work and accomplishments.

Be like the ants. When something pushes you down, tears down your dreams, or makes you feel like you've wasted time for nothing, just get back up, get started again, and make it better. You won't regret it.

Chapter 4:
DWYSYWD

"Close the distance between the work you do
and the difference it makes in the world."

Robert Cooper, The Other 90%

DWYSYWD stands for "Do What You Said You Would Do." Make a commitment, fulfill that commitment. Make a promise, keep the promise. Give your word, back up your word. Simple.

But let's talk about DWYSYWD. While we may, or may not, have already mastered how to set goals or build productive to-do lists, the purpose of DWYSYWD is about keeping commitments. These commitments may be related to goals or to-do items. But there is no requirement that these commitments be related to any major goal or to-do item.

When the number of commitments grow, the chances of successfully completing them becomes less likely. This is when DWYSYWD will work the best.

Use this method to DWYSYWD:

1. Write down the commitment you have made.

2. Write down the date that you made the commitment.

3. Write down with whom you made the commitment.

4. Write down the date and/or time you committed to deliver.

This list will become addictive. It will grow from something simple to a full list of all commitments you are making, whether work or personal, and you will become obsessed with tracking each task to completion. You will find yourself focused on meeting these commitments on time or early.

Use this process for everything. Big or small. Why keep these commitments in your head? Each of us has too many things going on day after day to retain any of our commitments in our minds. And with the digital age, we now have even more opportunities to easily track our commitments on our phones, tablets, or laptops. For those of you who still use pen and paper, there's nothing wrong with keeping a list on paper either.

Once people see you are someone who always meets a commitment and never forgets a promise, they will gain a great deal of respect for you. They will see you as someone they can count on to deliver, and they will feel empowered to meet their commitments to you as well.

Many people keep lists for things such as shopping lists, grocery lists, and to-do lists for home or work. This is *not* the same as a DWYSYWD list. While keeping a list is a great discipline, DWYSYWD is about fully controlling your commitment. Adding the details for the person you have committed to, the commitment details, the deadline date and/or time, you begin to have more control of your life.

Make the commitment. Write it down. Execute it. That's DWYSYWD.

Chapter 5:

Hey Joe!

"It's not about you."

Rick Warren, The Purpose Driven Life

My brother is well known for a silly joke that he has told for years.

Let me set the scene for you. A guy and girl are sitting in the lower level seats at a sporting event. People are everywhere. The two are talking, having a great time, enjoying some nachos and cheese, and taking in the event.

All of a sudden, a guy several rows behind them yells, "Hey Joe!" The guy stops talking, looks to his left, as far as he can see. Then he turns to his right, looking and looking. He turns back and starts talking to the girl again.

A minute or so later — same thing . . . "Hey Joe!" Same situation.

A minute or so later — same thing . . . "Hey Joe!" Same situation. By this time, the guy is getting frustrated. He has stopped his conversation with the girl three times now, looked around, and tried to see who is yelling.

A minute or so later — same thing . . . "Hey Joe!"

The guy turns to the girl — with an angry look on his face — hands her the nachos and says, "Hold these for a minute." He stands up, turns toward the back of the crowd, and yells "My name is not Joe!"

My brother told this "joke" everywhere he went. It was not uncommon for someone in my family to say, "Hey Joe" to my brother at family events, and he would turn around and say, "My name's not Joe!"

Whether you laugh at this ridiculously corny joke or not, there is a story to be told.

In his book *The Purpose Driven Life*, Rick Warren opens with four simple words: "It's not about you." The young man in my joke was sitting in a whole crowd of people. As you are listening to the joke, I'm sure you were thinking this guy's name would be "Joe." Why would you not? He kept looking every time the guy yelled, "Hey Joe!" But in the end, the punchline tells us the story. A story about a young man who has assumed that everyone was talking to him.

Now I don't think any of you would do this at an event. If you or I heard someone yelling "Hey Joe!" we would just assume this person was not calling for us (unless, of course, your name is in fact Joe).

Are you living in a world where you think it's all about you?

I'll be honest, our society has evolved to the "me" concept. As much as I have liked Apple products, they put "I" in front of each of them (iPhone, iPad, iTunes, etc.). We didn't even have selfies until just recently. But now people are posting pictures of themselves on social media everywhere.

I remember growing up — it *was* about me. I had to study to pass my classes. I had to decide what I wanted to study in college. I had to take that job so I could pay for my expenses in college. I had to decide what clothes I would buy, what car I would buy and drive, and what decisions I would make through college. I had to search and find that first job after I graduated, and I had to take care of myself.

But I want to share with you three times that I realized it was not about me:

- The **first** time I realized it was not about me was when my son was born. When he arrived, the doctor handed him to me. The way he looked at me was as if he was saying, *"Are you the dude who is going to take care of me?"* They say when you become a parent, you finally realize unconditional love. That was the day I knew I had to take care of myself, my health, my finances, and everything else, so I could also take care of him. **It no longer was about me. It was about me and him.**

- The **second** time I realized it was not about me was when I became a manager: The true passion in my career came when I became a manager, and it was no longer just about me. The situation was very similar to having that first child. I was now responsible for a "team" and not just myself. My decisions would affect them just as much as me. **It was no longer about me at work. It was about the team.**

- The **third** time I realized it was not about me was when I became a speaker. When I was growing up in school, I was very shy and so bashful that if people even looked at me, my face would turn red. I would have never believed that someday I would be a public speaker. But it happened. In 2012, I was asked to speak at a conference on software testing. Halfway through my two-hour session, I looked out into the crowd of attendees and noticed something awesome. People actually *wanted* to hear me talk. They were listening to every word, and their involvement motivated me. It felt like that moment, years before, when my son was looking at me on his Day 1 — as if to say, *"Are you going to take care of us?"* When I speak, I try to give each and every attendee something to take away with them. **It is no longer about me. It is now about *everyone*.**

Think about who you meet often. How can you make a difference in their lives? What can you do today to build those relationships and make a difference in someone's life, career, or future?

Intentionally focus on everything around you in every situation. Whether you are at work, a personal event, the grocery store, on vacation, or simply talking to a friend. Think beyond simply how this situation relates to you and more about how it relates to others and beyond.

But wherever you go . . . whatever you do . . . never forget, **"It's not about you."**

Chapter 6:
My Mom and Steve Jobs

"You can't connect the dots looking forward; you can only connect them looking backwards. So, you have to trust that the dots will somehow connect in your future."

Steve Jobs

No, I'm not about to tell you that Steve Jobs and my mom are my parents. But I do have an interesting story to share with you that spans things I have learned from both of them.

If you haven't heard the commencement address speech Steve Jobs gave to the graduating class of Stanford many years ago, you have missed one of the most motivating talks I have ever heard. His talk covered so many great stories and so much quotable material that I have referenced and used in my life through the years.[1]

One of the most memorable parts of that speech was Steve's story about how he was fired from Apple, and how he later returned to Apple as the CEO.[2] He talks about how this situation shaped his life for the better. In this speech he said, "You can't connect the dots looking forward; you can only connect them looking backwards. So, you have to trust that the dots will somehow connect in your future."

My mom told me the same through the years, as I was growing up. She has story after story about how one unplanned decision to be at a certain place or time would be something that defined the future of her life. She used to tell me stories about how she met my dad. It was completely unconventional. My mom's sister was married to a minister, and he was the pastor at the church that my dad's mother (my grandmother) attended. My grandmother arranged a blind date between my parents. This date led to courtship and eventual marriage.

Both Steve Jobs and my mom would have told you that they had to learn to trust the good and the bad times in life. Many times, we will face situations where things don't go the way we expect them to, but when we look back on the events leading to where we came from versus where we are today, we realize each of those things happened for a reason.

Each event, each decision, each move along the timeline of life can take us to completely different conclusions. I'm not saying things will always be positive and bright. But many times there is a "gut feeling" you feel deep inside you, and many times you're unsure whether to go with it or not. Trust your gut.

My path to speaking at events all over the world came from multiple situations in my life. After many years working in software development, I took a software testing course in Tampa, Florida. This led me to change my career focus to software testing. I updated my Twitter profile to show this change.

In 2011, someone read my Twitter profile, which then stated I was in software testing and wanted to write a book someday. This gentleman messaged me on Twitter and offered me an interview in a software testing article. I took his offer and was featured in my first software testing magazine with that interview.[3] What I didn't expect were all of the things that would occur after that tiny, nonessential event. I became friends with the organization that published the magazine. I began writing articles for them as well. I then began to speak at their software testing conferences in 2012. I grew from one-hour session talks to keynotes in front of large audiences, and ultimately became an international speaker at testing conferences all over the world.

What if I had never taken that training in Tampa, Florida? Where would I be today? Who would I talk to in my career and personal life? We will never know. I am grateful for how the dots connected for me.

Many times, a letdown, a failed job interview, a broken relationship, or an unaccomplished dream can lead to something better in life. Sometimes the negative event will open the door for a positive event. Many times, the alternative to what you felt was "the right thing" turns out to be exactly what you needed.

Whatever the situation, learn to trust the dots as they connect you to the future. Look around you as events take place in your life. Remember choices you make today can ultimately change the outcomes you see tomorrow. Evaluate what today's situation will do for you and whether it was exactly what you expected or wanted. Look out a little further and decide if you realize where this is going to take you.

Trust the dots.

Chapter 7:
Take Only the Good Pictures

"The art of taking a photograph is in visualizing
the picture before you take it."

Mike Lyles

My mom has taken more photographs than any person I have ever met. She is not a professional photographer, and she has never taken pictures as part of a career, but if you knew her over the years, you would know she absolutely *loves* to click pictures. Of everything. Of everyone. Of every event. To the point of driving those in the photos crazy with the phrase, "Just one more — hold on."

I am convinced that the reason I love cheese so much is, during the whole time I was growing up, I had to say it . . . all . . . the . . . time!

Today we live in a world where clicking a picture, selfie, photo is as simple as pulling out your phone, clicking a shot, viewing the results, deciding if you like it, and either accepting that picture or taking another one to replace it. So many of the youth today will never know the tasks involved in getting a photo developed. So many will never know the element of surprise involved in taking pictures back in the days of using actual film to develop pictures.

In the 1980s, to get a picture in hand, a person would load their camera with film. They would click the photo they wished to take. There was no preview to determine if it was "a good shot" or not. Additionally, the film would come in multiples of 12 (I'm unsure why 12 was chosen). A roll of film would have 12, 24, 36, or sometimes more pictures on it. Once your film was all taken up, you would wind up the roll in the camera, take the roll out, and in most cases, mail off the roll of film to be developed. This would then take several days for your film to be developed and the pictures to be printed and mailed back to you. Only then would you get to see the results. Anyone who took pictures this way can remember those days when you went to the mailbox to get the photos, opening up the pack, praying that the pictures were all good. Many times, you would open them up and realize someone had their eyes closed, someone wasn't looking when the picture was taken, the color was not right, the sun was shining too bright into the lens, there was not enough light in the picture, or some other issue. Back in those days, you could do nothing to fix this other than start again and repeat the process.

We were all in love with one-hour photo shops when they first came out. Many of us were willing to pay whatever it took in order to get this done. Suddenly our wait for days and weeks to see the results of a photo were reduced to simply one hour. We'd take the roll of film to the one-hour photo desk, leave it, and patiently wait for one hour to see the results. I can remember thinking how wonderful this reduction in wait time was for getting pictures. Being able to see the results in an hour was simply amazing. Little did we know, during those days, that only a few years later, pictures could be instantly in our hands on a mobile device.

For many years, my mom took way more pictures than she had time and money to develop. In my house, there was a bag filled with rolls of film waiting to be developed. So many memories went undeveloped and couldn't be viewed by the family. This bag continued to fill up, pictures taken but not seen. For over a decade, those pictures sat in the bag without any action. Then one day, the local one-hour photo ran a special. All film developed would cost only $1.00 per roll. My mom seized the opportunity and carried the bag to the store. She had 63 rolls of film in the bag and was able to receive hundreds of pictures and memories from the photo shop for a small cost of $63.00.

I remember that day so well. Our family sat around the kitchen table, sorting the pictures. Recalling and reminiscing as we looked over pictures taken so many years back. At times, it was difficult to remember where the pictures were taken and, most importantly, *why* they were taken. But everyone helped each other to recall the memory. It was so much fun to have memories of the past sitting on that kitchen table, reminding us of the good times, the many things we may have forgotten we had done, and seeing so many people in the pictures at much younger ages. It's quite funny how you realize, in a situation like this, that had we developed those pictures the next day or week, the importance of the event or how everyone looked in the picture may not have been that interesting. But to go down memory lane and recall those times in life that might have been long forgotten was something to cherish.

Through my childhood and early adulthood years, I remember so many times standing in a pose, smiling, and through gritted teeth saying, "Mom, why are you taking so many pictures? Why don't you take only the good pictures?" During those times, I used to wonder why she would click picture after picture, when I felt that one picture was enough to capture the moment. She would calmly and patiently say, "They are *all* good pictures, son." It took me many years to realize she knew exactly what she was talking about.

The ability to click hundreds of pictures and save them all on your mobile device or computer has given us the opportunity to *find* the good pictures. Today if I take a picture with my phone, I have the option to take multiple pictures in a split second and the mobile device will display the best picture of that set. Many people will never understand how easy finding that *good* picture is now compared to years ago.

As the years have passed, and I have experienced so many great things in life, I realized the phrase, "A picture is worth a thousand words," is so true. Trying relentlessly to convince my mom to "take only the good pictures," and receiving the calm reply, "they are *all* good pictures," rings in my memories each time I'm clicking the next photo.

With digital pictures on mobile devices, the cost per picture vanished. I realized that I began to click pictures of everything, pictures I would have normally not taken if I had only 24 or 36 photos in a roll and I would have to pay for them to be developed.

What does this teach us? What can we learn from the evolution of photography and clicking memories? My lesson in all of this is, Mom was right. They *are* all good pictures. There are no bad pictures in life. Every picture clicked is a frozen memory of one split second when we are alive and existing in this world. Seeing these pictures after dozens of years brought back so many memories of all the things that happened and shaped the life we live today. Too many times we are so busy with our work schedules, our hobbies, or our simple day-to-day activities that we don't stop for just a second to recognize all that is taking place around us. While the digital world may have helped picture taking to be instantaneous, it also sped up our lives to the point where we are constantly passing through life at 100 mph.

You don't have to wait until you see a picture to remember the good times and the great things that made you who you are today. You don't have to click dozens of pictures to hold the memory in front of your eyes. Take time each day to realize that you woke up this morning, you had breath in your body, and you were able to get up and live another day. Pay attention to things you may have taken for granted around you. Look closer at the events, people, and situations that shape who you are and where you are going.

Don't wait until a picture is taken. Live life to the fullest and enjoy each and every moment.

But most of all, always remember . . . they are *all* good pictures.

Chapter 8:
Who Will Win the Super Bowl?

"The measure of who we are is what we do with what we have."

Vince Lombardi

My favorite sport to watch for many years has been the National Football League (NFL). At the beginning of every season, I watch my favorite team, the Pittsburgh Steelers, take the field to rally for a chance at the Super Bowl. The Steelers were the first team to win six Super Bowls[1] and while this is a great fact, it's not enough. Any football fan will tell you that they want their team to win it all every year.

Whether your team is in the big game or not, the date of the Super Bowl has become almost a holiday for so many. There are people in this world who have attended every single Super Bowl since it started over 50 years ago.[2] People who usually have no interest in football at all will watch the Super Bowl due to the new and exciting commercials. This is a time when Super Bowl parties will be taking place.

In so many years past, I have either had a team there that I really wanted to see win the game, or, in many cases, there may have been a team I really did *not* want to win the game.

But as these two teams take the field, I see myself sitting back and just enjoying the game of football. I get to enjoy watching two teams go head to head for the Vince Lombardi Trophy. I have been known to be superstitious about the fact that I can control the win or loss of a team, simply by "willing" the team to win or "wishing against" the team I hope will lose.

This is a great metaphor for how we should look at events in our day-to-day life. Too many times we position our lives as if it is the Super Bowl and we are *required* to pick a team we want to win or a team we hope will lose. We see events at work or in our personal lives as ones in which we must either win or lose — and there will be no room for a break even or even a win-win situation.

Not everything has to be win or lose. There will be more situations in your life where you can collaborate and work with others and do something great. You have to be able to recognize those situations where it's not win versus lose.

Take a step back and examine how you approach each event in your daily life. Are you struggling with everything that is going on? Are you trying to drive things to a win at all costs? Are you subconsciously wishing for someone to lose? Does someone really have to "win" in this situation? If so, think about the situation and ask if it is truly important. Think ahead, six months, one year, five years, or longer, and then ask yourself if this is really important enough to be anxious, losing sleep, or worried about.

Think about how it feels when you are just sitting back and enjoying a game where you don't care who wins. Ask yourself what things you should be able to sit back and relax over when tomorrow comes. Or this week. Or this month. What things can you stop worrying about and let the "game of life" take its course? Focus on the important things. There are many things about which you *must* worry and you *must* win at. But if you truly look around you, then you will find the list of things in your life that are win versus lose is much smaller than the list you may have been working with before today.

Work the list. Every day is a new kickoff. You own the game plan for your life.

Get out there and enjoy your game!

Chapter 9:
Rudolph Was Not a Brown-Noser

"Strength lies in differences not similarities."

Stephen Covey

If you've lived long in this world, you have probably heard of the term *brown-noser*. If you've lived as long as I have, you have seen many brown-nosers all around the world.

In short, if someone is a brown-noser, they are using many skills to seek someone's favor. The person whose favor is being sought is usually their boss or someone in authority. The brown-noser will work hard to ensure they reach a goal (e.g., a promotion, raise, or other benefit). As you can obviously assume, the title of brown-noser is not a term of endearment.

Have you ever felt like you are not doing enough to get noticed and appreciated for the things you do? Have you struggled to determine what you need to do in order to get the attention of people who decide the future of your career or personal life? Are you afraid that trying to get attention will be seen as bragging or being too proud? Just remember, to move to the top, you do not have to be a brown-noser. Rudolph wasn't. And look how well this turned out for him.

Okay, I know Rudolph was not real, but let's have some fun with this story. Do you know the story of Rudolph the Red-Nosed Reindeer? Are you singing the song in your head right now? Here is a summary of the story:

Rudolph initially lived a tough life. He was different from the others. He had a red nose. All the other reindeer had brown noses. As the story goes, the other reindeer made fun of and laughed at Rudolph. Has this ever happened to you? Have you ever felt that others were making fun of you or not taking you seriously? If so, you can learn from the story of Rudolph — because he did not let this push him down. He remained persistent, kept a positive attitude, and kept going, even with adversity. He went about his day and focused on what he could do and what he was delivering.

The story goes on to tell us that the brown-nosing reindeer excluded him from their reindeer games, making him an outcast, and treating him differently than the others. In so many circles, those who are patting themselves on the back and self-bragging are getting the most attention initially. But it's not always strength and victory that win in the end — but instead consistency, resiliency, and dedication. Rudolph ignored the name-calling and the "better than you" attitudes of the other reindeer. He didn't get lost in the race to be Santa's favorite reindeer. He chose not to be part of the constant fighting to move to the front of the line among the other average brown-nosers. He stayed consistent. He did his job, and in the end, Santa picked him out of the crowd to be the leader among all of the others.

How do you handle being around people who work so hard to get attention? Do you go head to head with these people or do you ignore their attitudes and games and focus on what you can accomplish?

To be the best, you will find that you have to stop looking around and comparing yourself to the best that others can do. You have to stop worrying about what others are getting and how they are getting it. You must stop complaining that others are getting something you are missing out on. In most situations like this, you are only in control of where you are going with your career or your goals. Do not allow yourself to be so distracted by everything that others are receiving or achieving that you have no time to focus on winning your own race.

If you don't remain focused on what you can control, you will eventually get lost in the crowd and drown in the abyss of averageness. Focus on what you can do. Analyze your goals. Realize what you do great. Ensure that you are proactive, growing every day, moving closer to where you want to be. Hard work *does* pay off. The day will come when you will be rewarded for your dedication, persistence, and tenacity.

I know you may be skeptical. I've been there myself. We may think we have to be like others and brown-nose to get attention and everything else we want in life. The successful life of a brown-noser rarely lasts long. Their games will catch up with them. You don't have to be the same.

Instead of being a "brown-noser," let's try to be a "red-noser." Let's do our part to change the world. Inspire others to help us change the world, building a society where we focus on what we do great and how we can make things better. A place where we no longer make fun of others around us, but we lift others up. And most importantly, we don't let the negative impacts of others push us down and keep us from growing.

Red-nosers unite!

Chapter 10:
10 Things Your Body Is Telling You

"What you are speaks so loudly I can't
hear what you are saying."

Ralph Waldo Emerson

A few years ago, I wrote a cheesy little blog called "10 Things Your Body Is Telling You." I realized, while it was meant to be cheesy and funny, a lot of this can be taken to heart (pun intended!).

Enjoy these 10 things; laugh at the weird, odd, and tremendously cheesy way I played with words; but do not miss a chance to pull in the message each of these 10 things can give to you as a takeaway.

It's now time to listen to what your body is telling you. Below are 10 things that you should notice:

1. Each morning, when you wake up, remind yourself "ARM going to make a difference today."

Every day is a new day. Even if you have failed over and over, it does not mean you are not going to find success today, tomorrow, or in the future. All of the things you have accomplished in the past are behind you, completed, and you can start each day free with plans for the future.

I would be lying if I told you that every single day of life will be filled with major accomplishments. There will still be days where you will surely have struggles. During these times, you may not complete all you set out to accomplish for that day. But wake up with the positive attitude that you *could* make a difference, and focus on at least one thing you can do, each and every day, that would make a difference in your life, your career, the lives of others, or all of the above.

2. Don't let them say, "I TOE'd you so."

When I was growing up, I can't tell you the number of times my parents would give advice, I would *not* heed it, and later they would get to say, "I told you so." It's a painful sentence to hear because you realize that if you had listened, things would have turned out differently.

If someone is giving you advice, analyze the advice and determine if it is a reasonable suggestion. Many times our own egos tell us that we know better than everyone else. We live in a world full of people with many ideas. It's statistically impossible for us to have all the right ideas every time. Sometimes the best ideas in our lives come from those around us. Some of my best writings have been suggestions or discussions I've had with other people. Some of my most amazing keynotes and presentations have been from ideas someone gave. Some of my most critical life and career decisions have been made after taking the advice of others.

Never discredit the value of people in your life. Learn from those who have been there before.

3. Let the whole world EAR your "voice."

Through my many years of following great quotes, motivational talks, and speakers, as well as reading books, one of the best quotes I ever saw was, "Somebody somewhere is depending on you to do what God has called you to do." The author of this quote is unknown, but the message it gives is so powerful.

As I have traveled all over the world for events, and spoken with thousands of people, I have found that someone somewhere cares about what you have to say. I encourage my audiences to not allow their doubts and fears to keep them from sharing their story. Many people tell me, "No one wants to hear about my life or my story," but you'll be surprised how many do. Others have told me, "I am not sure what to share with the world," to which I always suggest, "Begin with a blog about what you did today, or this week, or this month. Watch the reaction of those who are reading your stories, and then grow from the feedback and support."

The bottom line here is, the world wants to hear what you have to say. Let your voice be heard. You have a very short time in this life to make a difference, and there are so many opportunities for you to change not only your life for the better, but the lives of others.

4. No one NOSE your potential better than you.

Through the years, I recall one great quote that always comes to mind when I'm around some overconfident personalities. The quote, from H. Jackson Brown, Jr., says "You can get by on charm for about 15 minutes — after that, you better know something." There are people who have a tremendous amount more charm than skill or potential.

Your goal should always be to present yourself with full confidence in the skills and potential you know you possess. Many people underestimate their potential. They let doubt and fear keep them from taking that next step to meeting a goal or accomplishment.

At the end of the day, no one truly knows what heights you can accomplish other than you. And chances are very good, you are not performing at the level you truly *can*. Take a moment each day to evaluate where you are, where you want to be, and what you need to be doing in order to reach your full potential.

5. Look around you for others who desperately KNEE'd your support.

Look around and you will find so many support groups, online support, customer service organizations, discussion websites, and social networks like Facebook, Twitter, Instagram, and LinkedIn. People need each other. The question you have to ask yourself is, "Who needs my help?"

When you begin to look for opportunities to help others, you will find there are so many ways you can contribute to the lives of others. You can volunteer for an organization. You can donate financial support to an organization. You can be a connector who will link two parties who have never met. You will be surprised with the results of your support once you begin to give to others.

The key thing to remember here is, it's not just about money. Time is precious, and when you volunteer and give your time, it pays high dividends. Sometimes someone just needs an audience to hear their story. Offering your time to simply listen to others is just as important as any other support you can give. Remember that sometimes people are not asking you for advice, but instead want someone to talk to.

Who needs you today?

6. LEG go of the things that are holding you back.

Procrastination is a dangerous thing. Nothing holds us back more than believing that we can "start tomorrow" and we put things off that we could be doing today. We easily find anything and everything to distract us from focusing on what needs to get done.

It is much easier to climb a mountain when you don't have to carry a ton of things. Don't let your past, your circumstances, and others in your life keep you from climbing to where you want to be. Take a long hard look at the things you do every day, and ask yourself if the things you are doing are important and helping you to get where you want to be. If not, then start stripping these things from your life. Strengthen your focus on efficiency and things that are important.

7. Keep telling yourself, "EYE can do anything if I only try."

The only way you will ever know if you will reach your goals will be if you start taking steps toward them. You will never win if you don't play the game. You will never get to the finish line if you don't take the first steps in the race. Whether you succeed or you fail, you will never know the outcome until you try.

The first goal is to know what you want to do. The "what" in this situation could be something small, something considerably large, or simply something you truly don't know whether or not you can accomplish. Regardless, you need to know this "what" before you get started. Know also "why" you want to do it. What is driving you to chase this goal. Why do you think it is important? And most importantly, you need to know "how" you are going to do it.

Know your passion. Know your reasons for doing it. You truly can do anything if you examine what needs to be done in order to achieve it. Don't let fear keep you from chasing the dream.

Get started. Rise above it all and chase your dreams!

8. Don't let failure stop you — NECKS time you will be better.

Many people who have achieved greatness did not achieve their goals on the first try. I have heard many great leaders in the world say the more you fail, the more you will succeed. Even when you are failing, you are learning something along the way. Failure becomes a stepping stone for you to determine what went wrong and the various ways you can correct your course and grow from it.

Don't let your hopes and dreams be destroyed by a failed attempt. Put the situation behind you and try again. Falling down is okay. The problem arises when you don't get back up.

Stay the course. You will get there!

9. You will never reach your dreams if you keep looking BACK.

The purpose of a car is to drive while looking ahead. The car's mirrors keep us from turning around and looking behind. Imagine how difficult it would be to drive a car if you had to do it backward or if you had to spend half of your time looking around you without mirrors.

Our past is something we can learn from. However, if we continue to worry about the past, and we stay focused on the events that occurred back then, we are at risk of losing the focus on the things we are doing today and plans for the future.

Don't let your past affect your future negatively. The age-old phrase "Today is the first day of the rest of your life" is one you should live by each and every morning. Learn from the past, and then leave it there. Focus on the future. Keep looking forward.

10. Follow your HEART — it knows where you need to be!

When you are evaluating where you want to be and what you want to do "when you grow up" (remember we are all growing up each and every day!), remember to follow your heart. Logic is a powerful thing, but sometimes it's a *feeling*. Sometimes you have to reach out beyond logic and go with what *feels* like your direction and future.

Don't let your mind overrule your heart without evaluation. Give yourself some time when your logical mind and your feeling heart are competing. Write down your options, look over them, and ask yourself which one means the most to you. After evaluating the options, decide which one you truly feel, deep down, will be the best one to take.

Listen to your body.

Chapter 11:
Stand Out in the Crowd

"I want to be different. If everyone is wearing
black, I want to be wearing red."

Maria Sharapova

One of my favorite songs through the years has been "The Luckiest" by Ben Folds. Ben shares a heartfelt love story in this song, and he tells us how he can see the one he loves standing out in a crowd of people. People who are in love will tell you that it's not always about the physical look of their significant other, their intelligence, what they have accomplished, how wealthy they are, what type of work they do, or their family history. Instead, it is a *feeling*. Something about their significant other stands out. Sometimes, especially with love and relationships, things simply work out because it is meant to be.

Beyond relationships and love, being able to stand out in the crowd can take a little more work. Even in situations where you hear someone say, "This person got the opportunity because they were in the right place at the right time." The thing we fail to recognize in this story is, the person who got the opportunity may have exerted an extra effort to *be* in that place at that specific time. The work involved to be there at that very moment is rarely coincidental or accidental. Sometimes you have to put forth a special effort to make coincidence a reality.

Regardless of whether you are an introvert or an extrovert, most of us want to be appreciated and remembered for something in some way. It does not matter whether it's success in business, bringing a new innovation or invention to the world, inspiring others around them, or being the best parent a child could ever ask for and want. The question we have to ask ourselves will be, "How do I stand out in the crowd?"

There are multiple ways to stand out in the crowd. Here are a few:

Recognizing Your Greatness

The first would be related to a phrase: "Figure out what you do best and do it better than anyone else." What are your skills, your talents, and the things you feel you are really strong at doing? What is something you know you are really good at? And most importantly, what are you doing to get even better at this skill? Greatness attracts attention. The first step is understanding who you are, what your capabilities are, and how you can grow. Greatness rarely happens overnight. To be great at something takes work, even if the skill comes naturally to you. It takes dedication, focusing on areas of improvement, and a tenacious core to exercise that greatness each and every day.

One Step Ahead

Wouldn't it be great if everything you did in your life matched your strongest skills? We are not always in situations where we are visibly better than all the rest. This does not mean you have to give up and be average. Being "one step ahead" does not depend on mastering a specific skill. Instead, it requires you to know what success looks like at every step. When you know that your skills are not the strongest, you can exhibit the art of teamwork, collaboration, and a passion to complete the tasks and, ultimately, the team goal. People notice when someone has a passion for greatness, and you have the ability to show greatness in more ways than just having the perfect matching skill.

Thinking of these two ways of standing out, you then have to define and plan your own personal way to stand out in the crowd.

What can you do today that is different? What are you doing that stands out? Do you understand exactly what needs to be done in your role or situation, and do you know what rising above average in this situation looks like?

It is also good to know who is watching and to know what they expect in this situation. When you are aligned with the expectations for any situation, you are now equipped with the ability to rise above it.

There will be days when you try with everything you have inside you, and still you may not stand out above the rest. This is not a reason to give up. So many great people in history could have easily given up, and we would not have the great inventions, books, innovations, and products in our daily lives. Being great and standing out will take some work. Whether you stand out today, tomorrow, or a year or more into the future, the one thing you must focus on is what you are doing *today* to maintain or prepare you for greatness.

No one is requiring you to be like the rest. You can be different. You can be creative. You can be better than all the rest. You can change the world. *You* can *stand out* in the crowd.

Stand up. Stand out.

Chapter 12:
Change Is Good

"Change is the only constant."

Heraclitus

Everywhere we look, we see change. We walk around with it in our pockets and purses every day. The small coins that make up the US currency are traded every day for the purchase of so many things.

Change is good. Not just the coins in our pockets, but change in life, change in your future goals, change in your current state, and most importantly, change in your path to success.

Each US coin contains the image of someone in history. Let's look at each coin and the quotes from the person depicted on the coin face.

The Penny

The one-cent US penny portrays **Abraham Lincoln**. He is known for many memorable quotes — one of which is below:

- **"Be sure you put your feet in the right place, then stand firm."**
  — Before you stand firm on what you believe, make sure you have evaluated where you want your stand to be given. In today's world, we are influenced by other people, social media, and the news. It's

okay to evaluate everything around you before you decide, but once you make your decision, stand firm on your choices.

The Nickel

The five-cent US nickel depicts **Thomas Jefferson**. Below are some of his quotes and takeaway points:

- **"Nothing can stop the man with the right mental attitude from achieving his goal; nothing on Earth can help the man with the wrong mental attitude."** — I strongly believe that before you can *be it*, you must *see it*. If you are thinking correctly, and you are using the right mental attitude, then you can accomplish anything you set your mind to. Before you take that first step, before you do the first task, and before you move in a positive direction, you have to be positive about your destination and think positively that you will get there. On the other hand, if you have a negative attitude, you continuously feel defeated, or you have established your plans in the wrong direction, then you will soon find failure. Constantly evaluate your mental attitude, from the beginning of your journey until you reach your destination.

- **"Nothing gives one person so great advantage over another as to remain always cool and unruffled under all circumstances."** — Wise words and, as most of us will agree, easier to say than to do. It's amazing, especially with the rise of social media, how disturbed and bothered people get at so many simple things in life. Many of us will allow situations in our lives to control our attitude, our emotions, and our reactions to all of the above. When you add another person into the equation, and that person is engaging with you, there is always a tendency to give them a piece of your mind or debate. There will be times when you must stand for what you believe and have a healthy debate or discussion. But if you evaluate the situation, you may find there is no reason to lose control or be disturbed. Learning to control your temper is very much like exercise. The more you exercise the control, the more in shape you will become.

- **"Determine never to be idle. No person will have occasion to complain of the want of time who never loses any. It is wonderful how much may be done, if we are always doing."** — Always be doing, thinking, planning, strategizing, and growing. Of all the things we can replenish, purchase, build, and manufacture, time is not one of them. Each of us will have the same number of hours each day. Take advantage of the time you have. I am not suggesting you work 80-hour weeks. The key to productive work is to work smart, not hard. It's not as important how many hours you put in as it is the quality of the work you are doing when you are actually accomplishing the task.

The Dime

The 10-cent US dime features **Franklin D. Roosevelt**. Below are some of his quotes and takeaway points:

- **"Rules are not necessarily sacred; principles are."** — Stephen Covey once said that we cannot truly accept change until we have a change-less core. This changeless core is made up of the principles that guide your life. Rules will come and go. They will be modified, adjusted, removed, and added. But principles are the changeless core, which you must evaluate for your life in order to be able to stand still and to grow. What are the values you hold on to dearly? Know yourself. Know when to stand for what you believe and when to compromise if required.

- **"The only thing we have to fear is fear itself."** — We will discuss more on fear in a future chapter. But my advice for you right now is to be strong, have faith in yourself, and never let fear infiltrate your drive to succeed. Zig Ziglar once said, "Confidence is going after Moby Dick in a rowboat and taking the tartar sauce with you." You are capable and you can overcome the fears and do anything you set out to accomplish.

The Quarter

The 25-cent US quarter portrays **George Washington**. Below is one of his quotes and takeaway points:

- **"Worry is the interest paid by those who borrow trouble."** — Anyone who has ever borrowed money knows the pain the interest charges will cause to the whole process. This is because interest never benefits the one borrowing. It only benefits the one being borrowed from. The same applies with worry as the interest on trouble. If you want peace in a time of trouble, stop worrying, build your confidence, and face the trouble without a worry in your mind. Because worrying will never benefit your troubles — it will only make them grow and become stronger.

The 50-Cent Coin

The 50-cent US coin depicts **John F. Kennedy**. Below are some of his quotes and takeaway points:

- **"My fellow Americans, ask not what your country can do for you; ask what you can do for your country."** — This is singlehandedly one of the most memorable quotes by any US president in history. Such great strength is found in these words. Whether you are talking about your country, your career, your company, your family, or your goals — you can simply replace the word *country* in this quote with any of these categories and it works. Begin *today* looking at how *you* can make a difference in all of these areas, and you will find the rewards will be extremely high. You have goals? Ambitions? Stop waiting on your dreams to just appear — start planning what you can do, every day, to improve your chances of meeting each and every one of them.

- **"As we express our gratitude, we must never forget that the highest appreciation is not to utter words, but to live by them."** — Many years ago, I read a book called *How to Become CEO* by Jeffrey Fox. One of his chapters talked about the acronym WACADAD (which stands for "Words Are Cheap and Deeds Are Dear"). Ever since reading this advice from Mr. Fox, I have tried to live by this principle. People don't care if you speak. They care if you act. Show the world that the principles and words you speak of are not just lost in the spoken word. Live by your principles and your words, every day, and in everything you do.

- **"The time to repair the roof is when the sun is shining."** — We have seen natural disasters hit the world. When writing this, I was watching on the news about hurricane recovery efforts for a recent major storm. The moment a disaster like this is over, the people of the impacted areas are focused on repair mode, working hard to recover from the impact of the disaster. They do not have the luxury of waiting until the sun is shining to repair the damages. In your life, you don't need to wait until you are in repair mode to start resolving the issues and broken dreams. Analyze your situation, determine the changes that are needed, and move on while things are in good shape, and you will find you are on the road from "good to great."

The One-Dollar Coin

The one-dollar US coin actually features two ladies: **Susan B. Anthony** and **Sacagawea**. Each of these ladies had memorable quotes — as noted below:

- **"Failure is impossible."** (Susan B. Anthony) — The day you set in your mind that failure is not an option and you aggressively pursue success at all costs, you will see changes in your life. Even if you fail today, you have the ability to succeed tomorrow. Don't let it get you down.

- **"Everything I do is for my people."** (Sacagawea) — There are many great books on servant leadership and serving others. The greatest sacrifice anyone can make in their lives is to understand the value of helping others and realizing the benefits of seeing a bigger picture, which is not simply about themselves. I realized a long time ago, that in each coaching and mentoring session, with the thousands of people I have worked with over the years, I learned just as much as the person I was coaching. I build bonds with my team. When we practice servant leadership, we can grow together by supporting each other. Zig Ziglar once said, "You can have everything in life you want if you will just help enough other people get what they want." Live by these values, and watch the miracles occur in your own life.

There are many types of changes we will face in our lives. Some change will be good; some will be trials. But all are possible to overcome and/or accomplish, if you have the right attitude and drive.

Mahatma Gandhi said, "If we could change ourselves, the tendencies in the world would also change. As a man changes his own nature, so does the attitude of the world change towards him. [. . .] We need not wait to see what others do." Great words to live by. What are you doing today to be the change?

Chapter 13:
Five Reasons You Should Stop
Pursuing Your Dreams

"Winning is not a sometime thing; it's an all the time
thing. You don't win once in a while; you don't do things
right once in a while; you do them right all the time.
Winning is a habit. Unfortunately, so is losing."

Vince Lombardi

Dreams. Goals. Ambitions. Everyone has them. Even those who say they do not, are, in essence, setting a goal to not have them. The question, however, is, what are we doing to reach the dreams and goals in life? What is stopping us from achieving the things we want?

I have spoken to many people over the years. I have listened to their goals, dreams, and ambitions. I have heard the excuses as to why they are not setting a clear path to achieving them. These experiences inspired me to compile a list of "Five Reasons You Should Stop Pursuing Your Dreams." I want to introduce something I call "**The 180 Look**." This means to take a 180-degree turn and think differently about the roadblocks keeping you from reaching your goals in life.

1. "It has never been done before."

Who hasn't heard this excuse? It's impossible. It's unattainable. No one has ever done it. Why do you think you can?

But you must rise above this negative thinking. The **180 Look** for this is simple. What if we gave this quote to some of the greatest achievements in history that were the first of their kind? Tell this to Neil Armstrong, the first man to walk on the moon. Tell this to Michael Jordan, one of the most famous basketball players of our time.

It's okay to be the first. Be thankful that you didn't have to be the first person to eat an egg or try milk. Those things took bravery. Don't be afraid to do something that has never been done before. You might even do something that no one else will ever be able to duplicate. Get out there and do it!

2. "You do not have the skills to do it."

How often has someone shot down your dreams by telling you that, no matter how bad you want to do something, you don't have the ability or the skills to accomplish it? Don't listen to these negative comments.

The **180 Look** you should take here is to remember skills can be learned, but having the heart and the passion to accomplish your goals is the critical key to achieving them. Feeling that nothing can stop you and obstacles can be overcome is more important than initially having the skills to accomplish the dream. You should focus on things that make you happy. Examine your life. Look at your current career, your current job, school, or day-to-day activities. Are you happy doing what you do? Is this really the direction you wanted to take when you think about your dreams, goals, and ambitions? If not, then keep looking — keep experimenting with the world around you.

Another point I will make is that through the years I have interviewed thousands of people to work with me. I have found, consistently, that people who have passion for the work appeal to me more than people who have the core skills. I can teach you or pair you with someone who can help you learn skills. My focus when interviewing people over the years has been to understand the core values that someone has for their life, how they work with others, what passions they have in their life, and how they learn.

3. "You're doing fine right where you are — you don't need a change."

By now you've probably heard the saying, "The definition of insanity is doing the same thing over and over and expecting different results." If you're stuck in a career where you feel nothing is ever going to improve, then think about change. If you're taking courses toward an education or degree and you feel it's not the right path for you, then change. And if you're sitting where you are, because you feel this is as good as you can get, but you know what you want to do with your life, then consider a change. But be sure it is something you are willing to dedicate yourself to and not give up. You have to be willing to possibly sacrifice certain things in your life to accomplish your ultimate goal. Your dream job does not always exist. Sometimes you have to build it yourself.

I heard someone say once that your Human Resources department is not going to set your career and move you to where you want to go. Your career and your growth depend heavily on the decisions you make and the opportunities you reach out to take.

The **180 Look** here is that it is important to periodically examine where you are in your career and life. If you are where you feel you need to be, then no changes are needed. However, if you are not where you feel you need to be, then let today be the "first day of the *best* of your life."

4. "You're dreaming of a perfect world — you don't really want to do this."

To be honest, this is actually good advice. It is important for everyone to examine if they *really* want to be pursuing their goals. Weigh the options and evaluate the pros and cons of where you want to go. If you still feel it's where you want to be, then set your sights on the accomplishment and get started!

Is there a perfect world? Probably not. But you can find a way to be in a world where you enjoy what you are doing if you search hard enough. The

180 Look is for you to find things you enjoy doing, things that make you happy and give you satisfaction when you have accomplishments. Evaluate whether you are good at it or whether you need more experience, training, support, or guidance. If your goal is related to your career, it's always beneficial to seek something in which people will pay you for your work.

5. "No one will ever support you."

Wouldn't it be great if everyone you knew gave you their full support for all the things you do in your life? I have bad news for you. It's never going to happen. Even the most accomplished people on the planet have had to rise above adversity, disbelief, non-support, and criticism. The **180 Look** that I beg you to consider is to never let someone else's opinion or criticism keep you from doing something you truly cannot stop thinking about accomplishing. Attempt to sell yourself to those who don't believe and show them it can be done. However, if they aren't buying it, keep moving on and enjoy the journey. Zig Ziglar said, "Don't let someone who gave up on their dreams talk you out of going after yours." If you look far enough, you will find there *will* be people who will support you. Find those people. Connect with them. Learn from them. Give them support in return. None of us is as strong as all of us. Find your support group!

Don't give up. You can do this.

Chapter 14:
The Drive-Thru Is Not Always Faster

"The fact that something is convenient does
not mean it is the best choice."

Mike Lyles

I am a foodie. I love food, I love all types of food. I love traveling all over
the world and trying the local food at each place. When I travel to a new
location, I enjoy searching for what the locals consider the best food in the
world. I would not consider myself a five-star restaurant connoisseur. In
fact, I can confidently tell you that while there is a time and place for great
food at awesome expensive restaurants, I have many times chosen a small
hole-in-the-wall restaurant to satisfy my hunger instead of a super nice
restaurant. My love of great food, and my passion for awesome desserts, is
so strong that I could write a book on my love of food alone.

What I'm about to share with you today is not related to my love of food or
interesting and memorable restaurants. Fast food has been part of my life
for many years. Through the years, I found myself working late hours and
deciding I needed to eat before I went home. The choice to buy fast food,
knowing it may not be as healthy as another restaurant, or make dinner
myself came as a decision due to starving on the drive back home.

With each of these decisions to quickly stop off and grab something to
eat came an overwhelming realization that *"The Drive-Thru Is Not Always
Faster."* Trust me when I say I have spent an enormous amount of time
studying this theory.

Here is the situation. You plan to use the drive-thru window to conserve your time, make your selection, pay for your product, and move on with your life. However, you find that you will be sitting in a long line at the drive-thru when there are no long lines inside the business.

When I'm reaching a restaurant with a drive-thru window and a long line of cars waiting to order, I always glance inside the windows to see if there are lines inside. If there are small or no lines waiting inside, I will park my car and walk inside and place my order. An extremely large majority of the time, when I leave the restaurant, I still see the same cars sitting in the line, waiting for an opportunity to simply place their order. If you have not noticed this, try it during your next visit to a drive-thru with long lines. You might be pleasantly surprised with how much time you save by simply going in.

I am here to tell you that this theory does not only apply to ordering at a restaurant window. It can be passed on to everyday life. How many times have we taken an approach we felt would be easiest and fastest, only to find we failed to notice that, in the long run, we took more time to accomplish the task. How many times have we convinced ourselves to "stay in the car" in an attempt save ourselves from exerting the extra energy to accomplish our goals more effectively and expeditiously?

You must be able to examine everything you are doing in life to reach a goal. It does not matter if your goal is to do something amazing in the world, or whether it is simply to buy something to eat at a fast food restaurant.

For each of these "goals," you must evaluate what you want to accomplish and determine each of the steps needed to get there. This should not come as a surprise to you. There is nothing forcing us to follow a defined pattern to reach those goals. We don't have to take Step A, then Step B, then Step C, all the way until we reach success. We are rarely locked down to a requirement that we must follow a predefined or expected pattern to accomplish our goal.

You must be conscious at all times that while a step in your path to success may seem faster and logical, it may carry risks that could delay or slow down your progress in the long run. Knowing you can get from Point A to Point Z without taking traditional steps is the key to being successful in everything you do in life.

One day I was waiting at the window of a restaurant and I shared my theory with the lady taking my money. She replied "Well, the drive-thru may not be faster, but it definitely is convenient and efficient for some people." I cannot argue with this. If time is not your concern, sitting in a drive-thru line is convenient, because you do not have to park, go inside, stand in line, and pick up your food manually. The drive-thru will always be efficient, allowing you to sit in your car, without having to move around or carry the food back to the parking lot.

The only problem I have with the convenience theory is, far too many people live their lives, work in a job, waste their time doing something they are not passionate about — and do so *only* because it's convenient. They are unwilling to give the extra effort to do something they really love, or to take steps toward a goal they have always wanted to accomplish. Please do not let this be your story. Never let convenience keep you from changing your life, improving the lives of others, and ultimately doing something great.

If you spend any time looking at great leaders, inventors, innovators, and people who have accomplished so much in their lives, you will find a common thread. This common thread is, they rarely let society or known facts or processes force them to do things as expected. Whatever the goal, whatever the outcome, these people *used* logic, but they never let logic force them to take an expected route to success.

I hope each time you are sitting in a drive-thru line, you think about Mike Lyles and his silly theory that "*The Drive-Thru Is Not Always Faster.*" Most importantly, I hope when you write down your goals for success, you think of my theory, and you take a few moments to evaluate alternatives and weigh those alternatives each time so you know you have a chance for a better way to accomplish everything you want in life.

I will say it again. Parking the car, getting out, walking in, standing in line, ordering the food, and taking it back to your car takes extra energy. It requires you to exert energy to do this, as opposed to simply sitting in the car and inching up to the window to pick up your food. However, this extra effort and your focus on giving a little more to accomplish your goal faster may pay you much higher dividends in the end.

Can I take your order?

Chapter 15:
Work-Life Balance Is a Fantasy

"No one ever said on their deathbed 'I
wish I had worked more.'"

Paul Tsongas

"Find your 'work-life balance.'" We've heard it all our lives. Everyone has
suggestions on how to accomplish this balance. The focus has always been
on finding a way to be successful at work while still finding the time to live
your personal life outside of work.

I am going to make a bold statement here today. Here is my theory. There
is no such thing as a work-life balance. It will never exist the way we have
defined it in society and business today. Even those of us who feel we have
a good balance between our day job and our personal life will admit to this
fantasy if we are true to ourselves.

I heard a character in a movie once ask another character, "Where do you
live?" The other character replied, "Everywhere!" This comical retort got
me thinking, this statement was more true than funny. Many of us, if asked
this question, would give a street name, the name of a city, or maybe even
a country, because we would be thinking about where our home is, or was,
physically located. To imagine that you "live" at a physical location is the
first issue in the mind-set that work-life needs a balance.

The myth we have created in our world is that work and life are mutually
exclusive. We see *work* as one thing we do, and we associate *life* with what

we do personally. However, the fact is, you are living your life no matter where you are physically. If you are at work, you are still living your life. If you are at home, you are living your life. If you are somewhere with friends or family, you are living your life. If you are on a business trip, you are living your life. If you are on vacation, you are living your life. Everywhere you go, there you are . . . living *your life*.

Instead of focusing on a *work-life balance*, try focusing on a **life balance** for yourself. Focus all your energy on every aspect of your life no matter where you are at the moment. Give everything within you for each thing you do. Go above and beyond being average. Your family and friends should remember you as someone who is dedicated, thoughtful, kind, hard working, and loving. Those who work with you should remember you as someone who is tenacious, dedicated, goal oriented, a team player, resilient, focused, hard working, and unwilling to give up.

Knowing how to make a positive impact in every aspect of your life and focusing on being the best everywhere you go, paying attention to the urgent and important needs, showing kindness to others, and prioritizing each and every aspect of your life regardless of whether it's work or personal will change everything. You will find that you no longer have to worry about "balancing your work and life," because your **life** will be what you do every second, minute, hour, and day. What you do during those days — whether work, family time, friend time, and all others — will be what makes up your life.

The focus of your life should never be whether you should work more or less. It should be whether you are giving quality and priority to the things in your *life* that matter the most, in the right order.

When this life is over, all that will be left is the memory of you. The question you have to ask yourself today is how do you want to be remembered. And what things can you do today to ensure you meet those goals in your *life*?

Chapter 16:
Time Does Not Equal Money

"Once you have mastered time, you will understand
how true it is that most people overestimate what
they can accomplish in a year—and underestimate
what they can achieve in a decade."

Tony Robbins

How many times have we heard the Benjamin Franklin quote, "Time is money"?[1] This phrase has been used for many years in business. When someone makes this statement, they are saying that every minute it takes to complete something comes with a financial impact. The more time things take, the more cost to do the work, and the less profit given.

However, in the real world, time does *not* equal money. While many people may value money as precious, there will always be an opportunity to make more. Even if you lose money, whether with a bad investment, a poorly guided purchase, or simply playing the lottery without winning, you can always find a way to gain money and replenish your debt.

When you lose time, it is gone. All you are left with is regret. When you fail to use your time wisely, there is no opportunity to regain that time later and benefit from a second chance at more time. Time is priceless. Time is moving at light speed. When you are born, you are given a limited and specific value of time for the rest of your life. Each day, each hour, each minute, the amount of time you have left is reducing. You are not given the privilege of changing your mind at the end of today and getting back today all over again. Time is precious.

With that said, there are some similarities between time and money:

- The value of time is how well you invest it. A simple change in the way you invest your time can produce favorable results. Remembering you have a set number of hours each day can help you to invest where you spend your time and what you will do with it.

- There will be occasions where you feel you are investing your time wisely, but you realize you made a poor decision in the investment. Do not allow yourself to be let down by this loss. As with financial investments, you learn from the experience, and you ensure you do not make a poor decision with your time in that direction in the future.

- With money, we set up budgets for ourselves, and we can determine where we are spending each month, and also, where we can modify our lifestyle to reduce the spend. With time, you can evaluate your eating habits and exercise routine and produce positive results to add more time to your life.

- Charity is a beautiful thing. When you give financially to special funds, there is a benefit provided by your giving. With time, you can volunteer support for someone or spend time with someone, and they reap the benefits based on your giving of time.

We should all evaluate our lives and determine where we can give time back to ourselves and our families — and to the things that matter most in life. Work hard, give 110 percent, but look around you and determine where you are wasting time and focus on eliminating those tasks and activities that are contributing to the time you are losing every day.

Spend your time wisely — maximize your time doing the things you love in your work and career, and giving you back time to do the most important things.

The clock is ticking . . . What are you doing today to change tomorrow?

Chapter 17:
Be There

"Be present in all things, and thankful for all things."

Maya Angelou

We live in the digital age, where everyone is carrying a mobile device with them at all times. All around us, we have television, satellite radio, online services for movies and special shows, thousands of e-books online, and all the music we could ever want to listen to available over the internet through mobile and computer devices. Apple suggested there was an app for everything you need to do in life. Now, years after that advertisement, there truly seems to be a mobile app or service for just about everything you can think of to support your life.

With such great products and services comes a need for responsibility. In 2018, Apple released an update to their iOS providing the ability for people to evaluate exactly how much time they use their devices. We simply have become so attached to everything around us, and the effect is so hypnotic, we do not realize how much the digital age is taking us away from real life.

Please do not get me wrong. I would never want to go back to the 1980s when I used to hop in my car and drive somewhere without a mobile device by my side. I would never want to go back and be forced to carry a large case full of hundreds of CDs for my music. I would never want to go back and be forced to carry a camcorder, a camera, and books around with me everywhere to get the same conveniences I experience today. How many of you have turned around halfway into your drive simply because you left your phone at home? I see all the hands raised.

With that said, try walking into a crowded restaurant or public location this week. Stand there and look around. Watch the people and how they are interacting with others. You will find people looking at their phones or devices. Or they will have on headphones with a call in progress or be listening to something on their device. You will see a whole table of family members sitting there together all face down in their devices waiting on the food to come. Go to a tourist location and take a look around, and you will find people focused on getting dozens of pictures with their phone. This is great for saving memories, but you risk being so focused on the perfect pictures, you fail to take in the world around you and appreciate the tourist site in real life. The days of small talk and socializing face to face are going away. That is, if we continue to evolve in the same way we have grown so far.

The digital age requires new responsibilities that require us to have such devices by our side. No one has to put their phone away and not carry it with them into a restaurant. We know going from one extreme to the other would be a huge challenge. But we have a great opportunity to limit the distractions and focus on the world around us.

The fact is, we have an opportunity to *be there* more than we are today. To all of the parents who have young children, you have to be there now more than ever. If you are not careful, you will realize your little babies who loved every minute with you will soon be driving cars, going to college, getting married, and having less time to spend with you. To the children who are now adults, give focus and extra attention to your parents and older relatives. Have lunch or dinner with them and focus on the moment. Someday you will wish you had that moment all over again. To the tourist who wants to take 1,000 pictures of each and every thing you are doing, find a balance between the pictures you are taking digitally versus the ones you are taking in with your eyes and your mind. The bottom line is, we must learn to *be there*.

I have been in my career for over 25 years now. One important aspect of a yearly job evaluation is to determine not only if the person *has* the skill to do their job, but if they *want* to use their skill effectively. I have found the most productive and successful people in business are those who know when they must *be there* and focus on the current situation.

The purpose for mentioning this is to suggest that you constantly look for ways to improve your focus, improve the attention you are giving to each and every situation around you. This is bigger than just business. This is bigger than just friends and family. It is a lifestyle challenge that requires you to apply this change to every aspect of your life. When someone is telling you a story, give them all of your attention. This is most critical when they have a problem they are sharing with you, even if they are not seeking a solution from you. When someone at work is sharing an update or work-related discussion, ensure you are engaged and giving your attention to the situation. When your children, parents, or relatives come to you while you are in the middle of something, ask yourself if the things you are doing right now can wait so you can direct all of your attention to them and focus on what they are discussing. Each and every one of us can *be there* more than ever.

Beyond the focus on distractions, the phrase *be there* can also be applied to service to others. Being there can be applied to giving your time and service to your family, your church, a club, or any other organization. We can do so much more to help the world become a better place. Even if you are donating today, giving your time today, there will always be opportunities to do more. If you are already giving your time and money to support a great cause, I commend you. If you are not doing this today, find that perfect opportunity to make a difference. My dad has always said that the more he gives, the more he receives in return. Through the years I have come to realize it is not about receiving a monetary reimbursement. It is about the personal satisfaction from giving without the expectation of anything in return.

So, I am asking you today one simple question . . . Are you there?

Chapter 18:
What Would You Do if You Were Not Afraid?

"Regret is the most expensive emotion."

Mike Lyles

When I was a teenager, I did not know how to swim. My friends had learned at much younger ages, and I was growing more and more embarrassed that I had never learned. I would still get into pools on vacations and events with friends. But I would never go into the deep end and would never consider jumping off the diving board. When I finally had enough of the embarrassment, I signed up for a swimming class. It was frightening because I was so afraid of failing. I gave everything I had and put forth the effort to learn. After several lessons with the instructor, I was terrified when she said, "Now let's try the diving board."

I clearly remember the steps to get me up on the diving board. I remember walking on the board and feeling it bend and wobble with every step. I remember the instructor saying to me, "You do not have to dive. All I want you to do is jump feet first into the water." Sounded simple, right? I was shaking inside. I wanted to do this. I wanted the instructor to continue to believe I was giving everything I had to learn. I stood there looking down at the water for what felt like hours. The instructor kept saying, "You can do this. Jump." After a few minutes of standing there and pulling myself together, I took the leap, and landed feet first into the deep end of the pool. My fear was gone.

Amelia Earhart said, "The most difficult thing is the decision to act. The rest is merely tenacity." Think about some of your greatest accomplishments in life. What fears did you have before reaching them, and how did you overcome those fears? Now think about those things you want to accomplish in the future. What fears are related to those accomplishments, and what can you do today to remove those fears?

We rarely get to see or know how the future will play out. Fear can impact your ability to make a difference in so many lives, including your own. Do not miss an opportunity to achieve a dream, a major goal, or greatness simply because you are afraid.

You are stronger than you believe. You are better than you think you are also. You have more within you than you think. And with a strong will and a dedicated attitude, you can do anything you set your mind to accomplish.

I was afraid to jump off the diving board because I feared I was not good enough to swim. But I took the leap and it changed everything from that point forward.

If you have something you want to do but you are afraid, document your options and the risks. Write down what you want to do, take note of the risks, take note of the consequences if those risks become reality, and take note of the benefits of success. What if you *do* it and you *succeed*? Do not let fear keep you from at least evaluating the options. You will never know what you can do with your dream or goal until you take the leap of faith. Go ahead and jump! You got this!

Chapter 19:
Hope Is Not a Strategy

"I didn't get there by wishing for it or
hoping for it, but by working for it."

Estee Lauder

Alexander Pope was quoted as saying, "Hope springs eternal." It is very likely hope has built a lot of dreams. What Alexander Pope meant by the quote was, it is in our human nature to hope for the best, even when things seem unlikely and impossible.

How many times have you heard someone respond to a question with, "I sure hope so." They truly mean this when they make the statement. In their mind, they are already imagining the possibility of success. There is a mad rush to the lottery sales counters when the jackpot reaches an enormous winning amount. People will stand in lines just to buy that one ticket that could possibly win them the millions, and sometime billions, of dollars. They watch the news and hear the reports, all telling them the chances of picking the winning number are one in millions. You will even hear some people say, "Well someone has to win it! It might as well be me." These people have hope. It may be a delirious version of it, but they have hope.

It is built into our human nature to also give second chances. How many times have you heard someone say, "I hope it turns out better *this time*"? Even with a failed past, negative events, and setbacks, we always hope it will finally work out this time. Now I would be a hypocrite if I tell you in every other chapter of this book that you need to keep pressing forward, learn from the past, and you will persevere someday, and then tell you that someone is wrong to give a second, third, or hundredth chance to something in the hope it will finally work. I am not naïve to the fact this may appear to conflict with my other suggestions and advice. I still truly believe hope and dreams are what give power to those who never give up and give success to those who learn from their past and grow. But the fact remains that hope is *not* a strategy.

Have you heard someone apply for a new job and afterward say, "I hope they select me for the position"?

Have you heard someone apply to a college and afterward say, "I hope I get selected to attend there"?

Or better yet, have you watched social media on January 1, and viewed all of the New Year's resolutions based on hope? Hopes range from weight loss, better health, exercising more, buying a new house or car, or getting a new job to a variety of other plans for the new year.

With each of these goals, the strength of the dream is built around hope. There is no denying that. I remember my grandmother laughing at me when I was young as I would tell her that I would so desperately try to control being sick by standing up and declaring, "I am *not* going to be sick today." There are stories in the medical field where terminal patients will be able to extend their lives many times by having a positive outlook on the condition. The magic of a positive attitude works because everything within us is connected. When you give up, your body knows. When you are optimistic, it knows that as well.

How do we turn hope into reality? Hope is only part of the equation. A positive attitude is only part of the equation. Knowing exactly *what* you want to accomplish is only part of the equation. Having that clear picture is fundamental to success. But none of these things matter if you do not have a plan. You must always be planning for what you want to achieve. If you were to say today, "I want to make a million dollars," you are not going to simply make it tomorrow. You have to set your goals. You need a "strategy program" to follow. Determine what steps you will have to take to get from

Point A to Point B and all the way to the million-dollar dream. Building this means you have to start defining those steps, which things are critical to starting, which things will be depending on the start, and which things you will do as you see success along the way.

When you start your strategy program, you must be tenacious and dedicated. If today you decide to lose 10 pounds, eat healthier, and exercise at least three times a week, then you must set that program into action. You cannot wake up tomorrow, decide to eat junk food, lie around, skip the gym, and hope things will magically take you to your healthy goal. Do not give up hope. Do not let setbacks keep you from pressing forward. I would be lying if I told you I have never had setbacks. But when you see success for a major goal or dream, there is nothing like it in this world.

Another important fact is how you deal with the steps that get you to success. While it will be critical for you to build your road map for how you want to get from start to finish for your goal, I strongly suggest you do not allow it to force you into taking each and every planned step if you realize a better path to success. This goes back to my theory that "The Drive-Thru Is Not Always Faster." As you are reaching milestones, getting things done, feeling happy and accomplished, you may reach a decision point in your life where you have to evaluate where you have been, where you are, and which direction you need to take to finish the goal. Do not be afraid to take a detour to reach that accomplishment. Focus on reaching the goal.

Set your strategic plan. No goal is too small for one. I think you would be surprised how silly I look planning each and every event in my life. Having hope is a wonderful thing. Having a strategic plan makes the good things happen. Don't lose hope. But definitely don't go without a plan.

I don't just *hope* you take my advice. I *want* you to take my advice and reach new levels of success.

Chapter 20:
Don't Die before You're Dead

"All life is an experiment. The more
experiments you make the better."

Ralph Waldo Emerson

It is so important you do not waste a single minute of your life while you are given breath in your body and a beating heart. You can do something each day to make a difference, enjoy your life, and leave a legacy.

Years ago, the country group Alabama had a song "I'm in a Hurry (And Don't Know Why)". The song talks about being in such a rush to complete tasks that we fail to enjoy the journey. How many of us are so busy trying to "get to the end" of everything that we do not stop and simply enjoy the moment each day? I have listened to this song many times, and I have concluded Alabama was not suggesting we just take it easy and cruise through life. The message of this song is that you can stay busy all your life, but don't be so focused on being in a hurry that you miss out on the enjoyment of living life each day.

There are people all over the world settling for jobs they know they hate going to each day. There are people going to school for degrees they know they do not want to work with. There are people in relationships they know they do not need to continue. There are people accepting their life exactly as it is, when they know that they can do and become so much more.

Many people will say, "I missed my chance," or "I am too old now — I don't have time to start this new adventure." Think of these examples of folks who started in their 30s and 40s:

- J. K. Rowling released the first Harry Potter novel at 32.[1]

- Jan Koum founded WhatsApp at 33.[2]

- Henry Ford founded Ford at 40.[3]

- Asa Candler founded Coca-Cola at 41.[4]

- Soichiro Honda founded Honda at 42.[5]

- Sam Walton founded Walmart at 44.[6]

- Thomas Edison founded General Electric (GE) at 45.[7]

- Jim Kimsey founded AOL at 46.[8]

You may be saying, "But Mike, I am no longer in my 30s and 40s" — well here are a few more:

- Gordon Bowker founded Starbucks at 51.[9]

- Ray Kroc started McDonalds at 52.[10]

- Arianna Huffington started the Huffington Post at 55.[11]

- Amadeo Giannini founded Bank of America at 60.[12]

- Charles Flint founded IBM at 61.[13]

- Colonel Sanders founded KFC at 62.[14]

- Fauja Singh started running marathons at 89! Amazing![15]

The bottom line is this . . . You woke up with another day today. There will always be something you can do, something new you can learn, some new gift you can share with the world. Forget about age. As long as you are alive, you have an opportunity to do something that leaves a mark on this world. Read more books (I'm grateful you are reading mine right now, and I am working on more, so please be ready for them!), learn a new skill, work with more people, get out there, and be alive.

You do not have to quit just because you feel you have nothing else to give.

You do not have to quit because your past is no good or you have failed time and time again.

You do not have to quit because you think you have done the best you can ever do.

You do not have to quit because someone told you this is the best you will ever be.

You do not have to quit because you think no one will ever accept something you would offer to the world.

You do not have to quit because you have already retired from a long career.

You do not have to quit because you feel you are too old.

You do not have to quit.

Get up. Get moving. You still have more life to live. Don't waste it by telling yourself you have done it all. Live every day like it is your last. Enjoy the time you have here. Do something today that scares you. Do something today that someone will remember.

Just do something.

Chapter 21:
What Other People Think of You
Is None of Your Business

"I've learned that people will forget what you
said, people will forget what you did, but people
will never forget how you made them feel."

Maya Angelou

In 1991, my sophomore year in college, I was blessed to be selected and honored as a member of the *USA Today* All-USA Academic Team. There were three teams of twenty people, and I was in the third team. This honor meant I was selected to be in the top 60, nominated by Phi Theta Kappa, and sponsored by *USA Today* and the American Association of Community and Junior Colleges. This was one exciting honor for me, because I was able to then, and ever since then, say that I have been featured in an article in *USA Today*. *USA Today* was our version of the "internet" back then. To be featured in a magazine or newspaper was pretty humbling.

Being spoken of highly is important to most everyone. Seeing your name on the news, in an article, or to be honored nationally is a great thing. The growth of the internet and social media sometimes takes away from the uniqueness in publicity, since it is now so easy to communicate all over the planet with one click on a website or app. Yet it still does not keep us from wanting to receive respect and support from others around us.

Alternatively, the growth of social media and the internet has provided the opportunity for everyone to speak more freely and easily about each and every thing that bothers them. We can check the news feed on any social media application each morning to know exactly how the majority of our friends feel about the latest news, the president, the government, their favorite sports team, some latest article in the news, or simply how they feel right there in their own homes around their family. People want you to see everywhere they are, with selfie posts, pictures of their food, what they did today, and why they did it.

But the most painful experience with the internet and social media is that technology opened the door for someone to more easily share with another person, and practically all of their friends, exactly how they feel about them. This causes major debates, publicly and privately, and people are really offended when others talk about them or think negatively of them.

Our society and culture advise us to dress this way, talk this way, work this way, do these things only, never do these things, and if you do not follow these guidelines, then you are not doing right. Our world suggests we must seek the favor of those around us, and if we fail, then we should do something to gain that favor back. We limit ourselves to things we feel are important to our lives because we wonder, "What will they think of me if I do this?" We force ourselves to work in a job, be friends with certain people, and respond in certain ways to events because we feel that if we do not do this, then we won't fit in. We allow the opinions of others to change us. Many times, we allow that opinion to make us people we know we are not. We have become a culture that wants to make sure we have someone's blessing before we can proceed.

Most of all, we have become a culture that worries too much about incorrect assumptions or opinions others have of us.

We have to be civilized and kind. It is a good practice to love others and appreciate everyone on this planet. It is also good to seek a positive outcome for everything we do and all those we meet. But do not let the opinions others have of you (especially the untrue opinions) impact you in a way that changes you. People get jealous of success. If you have not met these people, trust me, you *will*. Do not let others' jealousy beat you down and keep you from focusing on the success you want to reach in life. Do not let negativity keep you from growing every day and being the person you want to be.

Close your ears, focus your eyes on the goals, and let them waste their time talking about you. Don't look back on those who are talking about you behind your back. Leave them back there. Keep moving!

Chapter 22:
Are You Comparing or Competing?

"You were born to win, but to be a winner, you must
plan to win, prepare to win, and expect to win."

Zig Ziglar

In the 2016 summer Olympics in Rio, Michael Phelps, from the USA, completed the event winning four gold medals and one silver. He ended his Olympic career with 23 total gold medals and a grand total of 28 medals over-all.[1] He set the bar for all other swimmers with his amazing competitiveness.

While this was a remarkable thing, the story that gained the most attention during these 2016 Olympics was the competition between Michael Phelps and Chad Le Clos from South Africa. The world watched as the tension built up before the two competed in the 200-meter butterfly finals.

The story began back in 2012 when Clos beat Phelps for the gold in the 2012 London Olympics.[2] Following this defeat, Phelps announced he was retir-ing.[3] It seemed that Phelps would never race competitively again. However, before the 2016 Olympics, Phelps announced he was returning. With this return, he would take a different approach, one in which he simply ignored the conflicts and decided he would let his swimming speak for itself.[4]

In the 2016 Olympics, the pending event between Phelps and Clos was coming up. Phelps was sitting poolside, his coat on, hood up, staring into the pool. Clos began shadowboxing and appearing to warm up right in front of Phelps. Phelps did not break his glance and never looked up. In fact, he began to scowl with a face that would flood the internet with the hashtag #PhelpsFace.[5]

As the competition reached its time, the two took off for the 200-butterfly and were side by side, the world watching as two of the greatest in the event were going to take it down to the last few seconds. But as the race neared the end, a picture was taken of the two swimmers in the heat of battle. You see Phelps breaking into the lead, only a foot or so ahead of Clos, but that was not the most interesting part of this picture. This picture tells a powerful story. Phelps is looking straight ahead, focused on the finish line. The world is nowhere around him in his final push. To his right, you see Clos super close. But instead of looking at the goal and focusing on the wall, he is looking at Phelps.[6] We will never know if that one glance was part of the reason Clos lost to Phelps during this race.

When Clos chose to look at Phelps to determine where he was in the race, he was no longer looking at the finish line. He was trying to compete, finish his race first, but he was distracted by his need to see where Phelps was. Phelps was unaffected by the situation. It seemed he was not interested in where anyone else was at the time. His focus was on finishing his race, regardless of whether he won or not.

I used to have a quote on my wall at work that said, "Never compare yourself to the best that others can do." You may be better than some people, and you may not be as good as others . . . yet. However, when you set the bar for the limits that others have, you no longer give yourself the opportunity to reach above and beyond the heights others can reach.

Instead of feeling threatened and comparing the success of others to your own story, learn from how others have reached their goals and what worked and possibly did not work for them.

When I started to write this book, I interviewed some great authors, seeking to find how they found success. I sought to learn of their struggles, what things they did well, and what things they wish they had done better when they wrote their first book or started their first speaking events. Instead of feeling that I would be competing with other writers and speakers, I chose to learn from their experiences.

When you go to work or school or that event tomorrow, take a hard look at yourself and how you are engaging with others. When you arrive to start your day, are you feeling tense? Do you feel you are comparing their day-to-day activities with the things you are doing? Do you feel you have to size up your accomplishments with others? You must zone out everything around you, and keep your eyes on "your swim lane."

Choose to compete, not compare. And when you compete, do not compete with others, compete with yourself. Do something today that beats the person you were yesterday. If you continue this practice, you will find, in the end, you will be taking home the gold medal yourself.

Chapter 23:
Who Needs a Leader?

"The best leaders know when it is time to be big and when it is time to be small, so others can be big."

Liz Wiseman, Article on Forbes.com[1]

How many of you have played the game "follow the leader" as a child? We gathered as children, designated someone as the leader, and then everyone else was to follow the leader and trust their judgment.

Imagine how difficult the game would have been if it had been called "follow each other." Instead of a group of children behind one person making decisions with and for the team, you'd have a whole field of kids standing side by side and going in every direction. It would not be long before the game would become boring.

Years ago, I heard about a company named Zappos that was working on a new organizational structure called holacracy, in which managers have been removed and the team is empowered to work together.[2] The whole concept of holacracy is to build a stronger team bond and eliminate the need to have one person driving it all. The structure promises to fit better with agile teams, enable more autonomy to the group, and strengthen the decision-making process. This sounds exciting initially, but I struggle to believe that it's the most productive for many companies, because I firmly believe people have within them the need to be led.

Zappos CEO, Tony Hseih, was quoted as saying, "think of each employee with self-management and self-organization like a mini-entrepreneur."[3] With the organizational change announcement in March 2015, the company offered each employee the chance to take a buyout and leave the company if they did not want to work in that type of organization. Within 10 months after the announcement, over 18 percent of the staff took the buyout and left because they didn't want to be part of the changes.[4]

I'm honestly surprised it was only 18 percent, because I would think many of us want to have some direction and guidance. Even CEOs look for direction from their board members, customers, and supporters.

Why was this structure so difficult for some to deal with? I believe the reason is, it is part of human nature to be led. When we are born, we have parents who will guide us, protect us, and teach us how to deal with and survive in the world. We then go to school. We experience teachers, counselors, and coaches who provide guidance and direction for our education. Imagine how we would have learned as children had we gone to school and been told, "Work together, but we are not going to tell you what to work on, nor are we going to give you homework or exercises to learn."

As we grow up, we experience sports, and in part of that experience, we notice that a coach guides the team. I've heard the following quote many times through the years: "Players win games, but coaches win championships." We can all play well together. It's quite possible we can even be productive and successful. But to experience true success beyond all opportunities takes having a coach and a leader to drive toward the goals.

When I examine the holacracy practice, I begin to wonder why some people accept it and some people cannot. I have concluded that there are two types of personalities when it comes to how we see leaders:

The Leaderless

Some people do not want to answer to authority. They feel independent and want to have control over their responsibilities and their outcomes. Have you met this person? They will go out of their way to prove they do not need any authority or leadership in their lives. I have found that many times the leaderless individual truly *does* need support, direction, authority, and leadership, but they are stubborn, selfish, and they feel they can take care of everything on their own. I struggle to watch the leaderless push so hard to make their own way, when they could accomplish so many great things if they worked with others and took advice and direction.

If you're a believer of the "Leaderless" theory, then you must find the best approach to work collaboratively with your team to ensure the responsibilities are met without someone in the front driving the direction. It is important everyone understand the roles of the team. To be honest, even if you do not have a leader among you, there will always be a theme of leadership — which may be a "group leadership" process.

The Leader Needers

Most people require leadership and a push to keep them going. They seek guidance to send them in the right direction and drive them to success. Without it, they would simply sit and wait for the next suggestion or command. Even those who are leaders themselves need someone to help them at times. Having a leader to follow does not give away your authority or your ownership. It simply gives you a direction and support for where you want to go.

My advice to the "Leader Needers" is this: If you are the leader in front, you have a great responsibility, which cannot only affect your life, but the lives of others. I would assume many people are starving for direction to achieve their goals and success in life. If you are focused on winning with the team collaboratively (similar to the leaderless theory), while still driving the decisions and directions of the team, you can be part of something amazing.

But let's be honest with each other. For the reality check, it's very likely we live in a society where leaders are becoming soft. They are not accepting their position and driving the team aggressively with authority. Leaders who are not taking responsibility need to stand up and take charge. If you are a leader who does not want the role, or the role was forced upon you, then admit this fact and save the value of those you are leading. If you're in this position, maybe it's best for you to give someone else a chance to take the reins of the team. If you've ever seen birds flying in a *V* formation, keep in mind that the front bird is hardly ever consistently the same. Sometimes they fall back and let another take the lead for a while. You will earn much more respect by recognizing a change is needed than to just keep leading with no success.

Which best fits your idea of a high performing team? Whatever you choose, make sure you are a productive member of your team, organization, or group. We all have something to give, whether we are leading or following.

Chapter 24:
You Can Learn as Much from Bad Leaders as Good Leaders

"I've given up the terms good leader and bad leader.
You're either a leader or you're not a leader."

Simon Sinek

I used the quote from Simon Sinek for this chapter to share with everyone his take on leadership. In fact, I get what he is trying to convey to his readers and followers. However, I feel *leadership* does not always mean something positive. For years, we have seen this term used synonymously within a positive context, but I am not sure it has to be positive.

For example, many leaders in history led large groups of people to do very bad things. These leaders caused their followers to believe in them so much that they were moved to do things we would not consider good or positive. Many stories come to mind of followers who were so brainwashed by bad leaders that they conducted dangerous, life-threatening, and many times fatal acts upon other people, fellow followers, or themselves.

I agree with Sinek, however, that the art of leadership should always be praised when it is positive. There are many great accomplishments, teams, and events through history that have been positive outcomes due to great leadership. While I have not come in contact with the leaders who caused catastrophic and life-threatening events, I do have a lot of history working with both good and bad leaders. I want to share with you the many lessons I have learned from these leaders throughout my lifetime.

Here are some core fundamentals that the *"Good Leaders"* taught me:

- When you have subordinates working under your supervision, never say, *"They work **for** me."* Instead say, *"They work **with** me."* I had a former boss introduce me this way many years ago in a corporate meeting. I never forgot how that made me feel. Instead of feeling like one of the people who was lower and less important on the team, I felt part of the leadership team, and it gave me a higher sense of responsibility. To this day, I have never introduced anyone on my team as someone who "works **for** me."

- *"Look for ways to make your boss look good and your boss' boss look better. Don't let them make a mistake."* — This is one of my favorite chapters in *How to Become CEO* by Jeffrey Fox. This book has such excellent leadership advice. I was so inspired by this book when I became a manager, I bought thirteen copies and gave one to everyone on my team. The above quote from Mr. Fox's book has followed me throughout my career. You must always work hard to keep your boss in good standing. I have found when you genuinely do this, without any expectation of a return from your boss, you tend to gain tremendous respect.

- *"Nothing Fails Like Success"* — This quote came from Stephen Covey in his book *The 8th Habit*, and it has been a theory I have followed for years. This theory speaks to the fact that what is successful today may become outdated and unsuccessful in the future. It begs the question: How are we going to grow daily to stay in line with the ever-changing world? This applies heavily in technology and jobs related to technology, but it can apply to any type of job or personal situation. Keep growing every day. Do something today to be better than you were yesterday.

- *"I've learned that people will forget what you said, people will forget what you did, but people will never forget how you made them feel."*

— This is a powerful quote from Maya Angelou and one I have used through many years of coaching, mentoring, and training others. Think about these powerful words and how they apply to your life. We have had situations in our lives where, in the moment, we focus on what people say or what they do. But the thing that sticks with us long after the situation has passed is how we felt when it happened. Your goal in life should be to make those around you feel good about their interaction with you. If you are a leader, coach, or mentor, make sure you give people those moments where you praise them for a job well done and you motivate them to continue to grow. If you are a parent, remember kids forget things faster than adults, but they may never forget how you made them feel day after day. If you're working with a team of people, keep in mind you can be the one everyone thinks of when they discuss who is the most dedicated and considerate on the team. Think about how you make people feel around you. It is critical.

- *"Tell me what I need to know, not what you want me to know."* — This great quote has stuck with me for many years. I was working in one of my companies for a vice president named Tom James. I used to give updates to Tom weekly on the team progress. Tom had a tough job. He had so many direct reports at the time, and he was getting updates from everyone on his team during their one-on-one meetings. I tend to get wordy with my descriptions, and I like to tell a story. Tom was respectful and appreciative of my hard work, but he wanted me to know that he had limited time. This one simple sentence taught me how to improve my ability to give updates to senior executives on my team. We all want our bosses to know we are doing great work, while in reality, they already know if we are doing our job or not. We do not have to overtalk or embellish an update to the boss. We can get right to the point, summarize the key points, and make sure the message is given. All of this without taking a ton of extra time. I have heeded this advice in multiple jobs since my work with Tom, and I have given this advice to those who work on my team as well.

- My first boss after graduation from college was Nate Nixon. When I look over my 25-plus year career since college, I see dozens of attributes

I have instilled in my own leadership style, which I learned from Nate. Many people will go decades into a career, and even retire, without ever meeting someone who impacts their life the way Nate impacted mine. He taught me the simple things that have nothing to do with pay grade, title, work assignments, and financial benefits. Nate was a very special individual who taught me the value of human decency and how to show respect to clients and stakeholders. I never witnessed Nate lose his patience or temper over anything. I did, however, witness great respect and admiration from each and every client and stakeholder who met him. Nate had respect for our hard-working team. I remember on Fridays after we had a long productive week, Nate would come to me in the early afternoon and say, "Take off the rest of the day. We have accomplished a lot and let's start the weekend early." I learned how to respect my team and their personal time in every job since then. I have made it a point in my career to show respect and be understanding with my teams as they have personal time that needs to be addressed. Nate believed in me when I was just a rookie at my job, fresh out of college. He had no idea if I would succeed or not. He saw my potential, and pushed me to be successful. When interviewing thousands of people over the decades, I have focused more on the potential of the candidate, their core values and beliefs, and their desire for greatness, and I have done this as a priority over their skills. I can teach you skills, but I cannot teach you (easily) to be a good human being with good core values. Nate taught me early how to be a good leader, boss, and human.

- Another great boss in my career was Steve Shirley. It is very rare that you meet someone like Steve in your career. He was my director and I worked with him for many years in my company. Steve passed away years ago from cancer, but he left a mark on so many people in the short time he gave to each of us here in the world. Steve was known for his study of great leadership books. He had a photographic memory for the first sentence in every book he read. He felt that the first sentence was one of the most critical to getting and keeping his attention for the rest of the book. Steve spent so many tireless hours calling me into his office to share advice on how I could continue to grow as a manager, leader, and productive employee. Steve was tough. Many people saw the tough side of Steve, but just like a parent who pushes their children to do great, Steve did everything for me and the others on the team in the hope that we would grow and be great leaders someday. He taught me the value of being friends with those who work with you, while also making sure they understand your authority and role in the organization. I cherished the fact that I got to meet and know Steve for so long, and while I was not working with him in the final year of his life, I stayed in touch with him up until the last days. I will never forget the impact he had on my life. *You* can be that Steve Shirley to others. Work hard to be that boss everyone talks about when asked, "Who was your favorite boss of all time?" I have made it a top goal of mine to be "That Boss" who people think of when asked this question. I am inspired when I hear those who work with me say I am their choice.

And here are some core fundamentals the *"Bad Leaders"* taught me:

- First of all, I respect each and every person I have worked with over the years too much to call out specific names in this section. But I will say two things for those leaders who were bad. First, you know who you are. And second, it inspires me that after all we went through, you are now reading my book! Life is funny sometimes, right?

- Never be a hypocrite. — People will remember if you stand firm on a topic or situation but you easily change your stance without any real reason. Stand as strong as you wish on your core beliefs and what you feel is the right thing, but do not easily toggle between those beliefs and make yourself look unstable. There *will* come a time when you will likely have to make a decision or a take stand on something from a different angle. But when this time comes, be sure to acknowledge that you realize this has happened, and give reasons for why you had to change your stance.

- Vince Lombardi said, "Praise in public, criticize in private." I firmly believe in this. If you are a leader and your team is right and doing a great job, make sure you recognize them for a job well done and let the rest of the team and other teams around you know this as well. If they are wrong and they need to be corrected in the situation, do not criticize and correct this in public. Take the person to the side, one-on-one, and give them your input. But beyond this quote, I give an additional word of advice. And that is, do not tell someone they are amazing and doing a great job when you know they are not. Never give the positive feedback so strongly if the person needs to focus on an area and they are not doing well. Keep it in your mind, take it offline, and talk to them. They deserve to know they have work to do in order to improve. Fake positive feedback will ensure this person never knows where they need to get better.

- Don't show favorites. — Any parent will tell you that if you have multiple children and you show favoritism, then you begin to shut out the others, and the respect they have for you as a parent will slowly diminish. There is nothing wrong with making your team feel good. There is nothing wrong with praising each and every one of them. And as mentioned above, you praise them when they deserve it. But this does not mean you are going to be able to pick one or two from the team and give them favoritism. It will not only cause the team to lose respect for you as a leader, it will cause them to resent and disrespect the work of their teammates. As with parenthood, it is okay to acknowledge that you really like one person and the work they do a lot, but it is not advisable to show that favoritism in front of everyone.

- Give the team courage, not fear. — There are leaders and bosses who use authority and fear to drive their teams. This works, but only for a short time. Eventually people will be worn out by fearing you as the leader. They will talk about you behind your back. They will wonder why you can't be respectful and lead with courage instead of fear. If you are a leader and you continuously inflict fear on the team, your team will begin to drop out and move on to somewhere else.

- Control your emotions. — There will be times when things at work get ugly and unpleasant. Focus on controlling your emotions when you are working with a team, especially if you are the leader. Your behavior in each and every situation will be driven down to your team. Your followers will mimic your emotions. I can almost always tell the type of leader in a group by looking at how the others on the team interact and engage with me. Be that leader who shows you are in control not only of the situations but also of your emotions.

- Don't dwell on the politics. — After decades in the corporate world, working for multiple organizations, I feel that I have seen every type of leadership style and every type of event that could happen in someone's career. The one thing that has plagued many organizations where I have worked is the politics of work. This becomes critical to understand when you are in the workplace. You have to know who is playing fair, who is playing dirty, what the rules are, what matters most to the organization, and what matters least. The issue for bad leaders is getting so caught up in the politics that they focus on playing the game and forget the goals and mission of the organization. I will not lie to you. I have seen many people grow in their career playing the political game. But I have seen more of them fail in the long run, because they are unable to sustain this game. My advice to you is to refrain from the politics. Do your job, work with your boss to understand the mission and goals of the company, and let your work speak for itself. Let karma take care of the rest.

You may have read through each of these and said, "Mike, you *do know* that leadership and management are not equal definitions, right?" Yes, I know this fully. I also know that you can be a leader whether or not you are in a manager role. I did take a lot of ideas for good and bad leaders from management teams that I have encountered over the years, but I feel that these qualities and traits surpass the management title.

I am thankful to both the good leaders and the bad leaders in my life. Both groups taught me valuable lessons. My leadership style has, for decades, been one that combines the good things I've learned and the focus on making sure I deny myself the chance to give any of the bad things to my teams.

Learn from every experience you have. Good or bad. Grow yourself to be the best of both!

Chapter 25:
Slower Traffic Keep Right

"There are plenty of difficult obstacles in your path.
Don't allow yourself to become one of them."

Ralph Marsten

In the United States, an interesting sign exists on many of the multilane interstate highways. The far-left lane is used for passing the slower vehicles, and has even been called "the passing lane" or "the fast lane" for years. This sign simply states "Slower Traffic Keep Right." The purpose of this sign is to request those in the far-left lane be respectful and stay to the right so faster moving vehicles can pass them and keep moving to wherever they are going.

I have witnessed many times when a driver takes up the left lane, driving slowly and holding up traffic behind them. When traffic is heavy, this begins to impact drivers wanting to move faster and farther down the road.

Those behind the slow driver have responded in various ways. From followers flashing their lights at the left-lane driver, requesting kindly for them to move out of the way, to full-contact road rage.

To all of the left-lane drivers out there, I simply want to say, "Please move over and let the rest of us go on." It is a common courtesy and, in many states of the US, a way you can avoid getting a moving violation from law enforcement. It also keeps those aggressive and impatient drivers from losing their minds.

There is nothing wrong with enjoying a drive along the highways at whatever speed you wish to drive. The only advice here is to not allow your speed or driving in the left lane to impact others who may not have the convenience of waiting on you to move out of the way.

How can we apply this theory to our everyday lives? Quite simply. We all have things we want to accomplish in our lives. Some of us have very large goals with major tasks that must be completed daily, weekly, and monthly, to reach where we want to be. Some of us have small goals, with smaller, but just as important, tasks to complete. The pace we set for ourselves may or may not be the pace of others on our teams, in our family, or in our community circles. It is absolutely okay for each of us to set that pace ourselves and drive to our goals in the lane we choose. However, we stand to cause issues when we are sitting in the "left lane" and holding up the progress of others who need to move on and reach the goals and tasks they have set to accomplish.

Never let the pace and accuracy of the work you do every day be the reason someone else is unable to be successful with their plans. Never sit in the "left lane" and cause others to lose momentum in the things they have set out to do. Collaboration with teams at work, family members, friends, and community can build great success for each aspect of your life. But the challenge is to never be the weakest link who is holding up production.

I have seen this issue many times with sports teams. You find one arrogant superstar who feels they are not getting what they deserve. This star begins to slow down, cause debates and conflicts in the locker room, raising all sorts of concerns publicly about the team, the coaches, and the owners. Eventually this begins to impact the whole team. Many times, it causes them to lose in competitions. One simple, inconsiderate, thoughtless set of acts, and multiple lives and teams are impacted. It does not have to be this way. If only those players who feel they deserve to be in the way would simply move out of the way and let the others move on without them, we would see a change in the way that team plays together in the future. You begin to see more wins, more collaboration, and more success.

Whether it is on a sports team, in the office, at home, or simply with friends, the common courtesy of staying "out of the way" allows great things to happen. As with driving in the left lane, the decision to simply move out of the way is, so many times, such a simple thing to undertake.

Don't hold others up in the "left lane" of your life. Move over, drive alongside them, but let them keep moving on, even if they move faster and leave you moving at your own pace.

Buckle up. Drive safe. Watch out for those who are moving fast. Safe travels.

Chapter 26:
The Fastest Car Doesn't Always Win the Race

"Done is better than perfect."

Sheryl Sandberg

What book written by a North Carolina born and raised resident would be complete without a chapter related to NASCAR? For anyone reading my book who is either not from the USA (I hope this is reaching all over the planet), or who *does* live in the USA but is not familiar with the term NASCAR, I will tell you a little more about it. The National Association for Stock Car Racing (NASCAR) began many years ago with drivers running from law enforcement to sell and distribute a product called "moonshine" (a bootleg version of whiskey in those days). Through the years, the bootleggers improved their cars in order to evade the police, and eventually the sport took off with fans watching race car drivers compete on a race track at multiple locations throughout the southern United States.[1]

I have attended multiple races in my lifetime. It is exciting to see cars running at average speeds greater than 175 miles per hour around the track. Hardcore fans will tell you that the race becomes more exciting when you see crashes and wrecks during the race. This adds to the excitement when you watch drivers attempt to dodge the action when one of the front cars makes a mistake, spins out in a turn, or hits the side walls and begins veering back into the traffic.

The races consist of various tracks throughout the country with differing lengths. But every race runs hundreds of laps, which usually moves along fast when cars are racing at such high rates of speed. The cars are all set up to run close to the same speeds, which then forces the drivers to be competitive and strategic about how they move around the track. Their decisions are critical for when they want to make a move to get to the front of the pack. And they have to be quick to react when they see trouble on the track, which may cause them to wreck or be pushed farther back in the line of cars.

Each race team has a pit crew. These crews are all located in the center of the race track, and there is a "pit row" where cars can take an exit off the race track anytime during the race, and get a race car version of car maintenance service. I find it very exciting to watch the crew run out when their car arrives, a couple of people changing tires in just a few seconds, one person holding a large gas can up to fill the car with gas, one person cleaning the windshield, and others doing whatever it takes to get the car back in shape. In the event that the car has an accident, picks up debris from the track, or has engine troubles, the driver can come in for a more detailed maintenance update from the pit crew.[2]

As you can see, being a NASCAR driver, team, and pit crew takes both a tactical plan and a strategic plan to be successful. I have seen drivers make modifications in the pit to try to improve their speed and accuracy on the track. Sometimes the chance of winning lies solely in how well the pit crew and the race team plans for each event that happens during the race.

Many times, one car will lead the rest for most of the race, and then something happens near the end that takes them out. We have seen cars lose a tire due to a punctured hole. We have seen the leader getting so far ahead of the rest that they reach the slower cars at the end of the pack — these less experienced drivers may not know how to get out of the way and this can cause a collision. We have seen leaders run out of gas in the last lap. We have seen other cars in 2nd, 3rd, 4th, and other top 10 places trying to work their way to the front of the pack in the last couple of laps left in the race, and in that frustration and aggression, one tiny slip, and all the cars in the front are wrecking and hitting the wall.

What I have seen time and time again is a simple theory: the fastest car does not always win the race. The drivers who win the race are consistent.

They play the race strategically, watch out for trouble, make sure they focus on good pit stops, and when they see an open opportunity, they take it to move to the front.

In addition to the strategy and tactics, I have found it exciting to watch emotions get the best of drivers who decide to fight each other.[3]

How can you apply this theory to your life? It is quite simple. You are competing in a race everywhere you go. Whether you are at work, at school, around friends and family, or just in a race against yourself. All around you people are seeking and finding success, whether it is working around their home, completing a school assignment, getting that scholarship you wanted for yourself, getting that job you wanted for yourself, buying that new car or house that you wish you could afford, or simply finding a way to succeed in every aspect of their lives.

You must stay the course. Keep working hard, working consistent, and stay focused on your goal. What do you want to accomplish with your life? What things are important to you? Everyone has good days and bad days. Do not let those who are leading in your race cause you to give up. Don't tell yourself that you will never be in the front. All it takes is one setback, one turn of events, one bad decision on the leaders, and you are in the front, leading the rest, and showing everyone how it looks to win.

Consistency is the key. You do not have to lead the race for all 500 miles. You just need to be in the front on mile 500 of 500. I started putting together notes on a book in 2002. I have watched some great people write the most beautiful books on leadership and motivation. I have watched friends and family be successful in reaching their goals much faster at times. I won't lie to you. I gave up completing this book thousands of times, but I never gave up on the dream. It took me 17 years to write the last chapter of this book, and my drive to never give up and keep working hard to finish has paid off after all the years of sticking with it and giving a little every month and year.

What are you dreaming about in your life that you want to do? What big goal do you have that you feel others are going to reach, invent, complete, or be successful with long before you can do it yourself? Please don't give up. Please don't stop believing in yourself. It doesn't matter if it takes you a year, 2 years, 5 years, or 17 years like me —you never have to give up. Stay *on track*. Watch out for the wrecks in life. Make sure you build a good "pit crew" around you that will support you, give you direction, help you stay on track, and win the race.

Your time is coming. It doesn't matter what position you are in right now in the race. What matters is that you *finish strong*.

Chapter 27:
Are You a Factory Worker?

"Your career is what you're paid for. Your
calling is what you're made for."

Steve Harvey

My dad is a wonderful man. I realized, after I grew up and became a father myself, exactly how much he provided for my family, as well as the sacrifices he made so I could have the things I needed in life. He is one of the most unselfish and giving people you could ever meet. You have surely heard many people say, "I want to give more to my children than I received when I was growing up." My dad made this a difficult task for me to accomplish. Because I realized, after becoming a parent, the thing you "give" to your children is more than just buying them everything they want and having the money to provide everything for them. It is truly about the core values that you live, the way you perceive life, and the fundamentals of being a good person. That means more than any price tag you can place on the things you receive in this world. My goal is to be half the father to my children that my dad was for me.

Now that I am an adult, I realize the many times my dad gave me money when he had to go without something in his life. I realize the times he trusted me to drive his vehicles, never expressing one ounce of fear that my young, untrained, immature experience in driving would be a worry for him. He did not expect anything in return for what he gave to me and my brother, and he will never know how much that meant to me when I look back on it.

My dad was a man of many talents when I was growing up. At one time, he was a part-time policeman for the local police station. Nothing is more exciting than getting to ride with your dad in a police car. You realize when you grow up that it is much more fun as a kid than as an adult — am I right? He took a job at Sears as manager in the automotive department. He became widely known all over the town and neighboring towns as the man to go to if you needed new tires or your car serviced. He became somewhat of a celebrity in this job, as many would send word to their friends and family to service their cars with him as well. Keep in mind, this was the 1980s. Social media back then was a phone call or a post in a newspaper. He loved this job, and he enjoyed the interactions he had with returning and new customers.

I remember the day Sears decided to close down their automotive department in town. I remember this day because I had never seen my father cry the way he cried when he came home to tell the family he would be losing his job and he was not sure where he would go next. I remember sitting in my room as my mom consoled him in the other room. I remember feeling helpless, wanting to know how I could help him. No one wants to hear their parents crying in such agony. I realized how much he loved his work, and most of all, how much he wanted to support our family and be the best he could be for everyone.

Then the sun came out. Life began to smile upon my dad right away. He took a job as a manager with a nearby factory, and he began what would become a very long career for himself. He made so many great friends. He studied for the machines he worked on. He received award after award each year for the job he did. He found his "work home" with this factory. The company had a family atmosphere.

This was an exciting job for my dad, because he worked three consecutive days on, and then took three consecutive days off. His work schedule always rotated. This made planning family events interesting because you always had to know his schedule in order to plan things. During his days off, he became an entrepreneur, started his own archery store, and ran this store for many years. He employed our family to support this store for days when he was at work. He did not settle with just going to the factory every day. He used his free time to do so many other things.

The factory my dad worked for saw changes, buyouts, and acquisitions through the 33 years my dad was with them. But he stuck with it, and we celebrated his retirement right there in the break room of the factory. I got to witness the lives he touched in his role, as coworkers in the factory came up to him, one by one, and wished him the best in retirement. I watched other friends sadly say good-bye to him and tell him they would keep in touch. I got to witness my mom, celebrating, because she knew she would no longer have to wait for him to come home from work anymore. All was well with the world.

Why am I telling you all of this? Did I want to just tell you another family story? The answer is no. I began using the term *factory worker* many years ago to describe when someone is just doing the basics. They are going in, punching the clock, doing the routine, watching the clock tick the hours away, finishing their shift, punching out of the clock, and going home. I mean no disrespect to anyone who is currently a factory worker, has ever worked in a factory in the past, or has family who worked in a factory. There is nothing at all derogatory to be said about being a factory worker. In fact, pride can be taken in the role. What I want you to take from this is, you do not have to follow a routine. You do not have to just get up, go to work, do the same thing, and go home. You can be different, even if you literally work in a factory like my father. He stepped outside of the box. He was different. He learned new ways to do his job. He engaged with others, built strong connections and friendships, and gave everything he had to be successful.

Regardless of your occupation or career, you do not have to be a *factory worker.* Even if you say to me that you are retired, or you are a teenager without a job, or you are simply between jobs right now, this theory will work for you as well. With everything you do in life, you do not have to go by a script. You do not have to do the same routine every day. You do not have to wake up every morning with a plan to do the same thing over and over, and close the day with a repeated set of tasks complete. You can study, you can plan, you can look for new things to do, new things to study, new and exciting tasks for your day. You can grow each and every day by following this method:

- Are you in a technical role where you are providing a service to your company? If so, what things can you learn after work, on the weekends, that will help you to be amazing at your job? What connections can you make out in the world, on social media, in the technical community, that you can learn together and become a superstar?

- Are you a student in school who feels you are just going to class every day, learning a little at a time, but not becoming the best you can be? Look for more things to read online, buy some new books on subjects that you like, get out there and meet people who have the same passion and likes as you do. Social media is great, but please do not sacrifice the benefits of face-to-face interaction with others for an app or being online. The fact that you are in school does not mean you cannot be planning for greatness after graduation.

- Are you retired and feeling like you have already done everything you can do in life? I am sorry, but you are not done yet. You have plenty to give to the world. In fact, now is the best time to do everything you always wanted to do but never got a chance in the past. You woke up this morning. You got out of bed. Now what are you going to do with this new day? If you can think of nothing else, I suggest you teach someone younger something they can take with them in their lives. Nothing beats experience in this world. You have probably lived more experiences than some of the younger generation will ever see in their lifetime. Share with others how you made it. You will be surprised the difference it can make.

Maybe you're not in a technical role at work. Maybe you're not a student or someone who is retired. I could sit here and go through every possible role and job and we would have a book full of suggestions. But I will summarize all the others in this one paragraph. Whatever you are doing, whatever your current state in life, wherever you are in this world with whatever job (or no job), you can change the daily routine. Do not allow yourself to become complacent and accept that you do the same steps every day and follow the same routine every day. Even if you only study one thing, or do one new activity every day, each and every new thing you do makes you grow a little more.

If you are a leader, in whatever job or organization you are in, you have a great responsibility as well. I relate this to being a parent. Once you become a parent, you no longer are only responsible for *your* life, but now you are responsible for *your* life and the lives of *others*. Being a leader means not only looking for ways to make yourself grow, but to also give advice, coach, mentor, and train others, under your direction, on how they can grow as well.

What will you do today to step outside of the box?

Chapter 28:
Keep a Diary

"Owning our story can be hard but not nearly as difficult
as spending our lives running from it. Embracing our
vulnerabilities is risky but not nearly as dangerous
as giving up on love and belonging and joy—the
experiences that make us the most vulnerable. Only
when we are brave enough to explore the darkness
will we discover the infinite power of our light."

Brené Brown, The Gifts of Imperfection

In the introduction of this book, I mentioned that beginning July 2002, I started to take notes on leadership, motivation, quotes, and other interesting things in my life. I realized back then that my life was going to take me in so many awesome directions, I was going to meet so many great people, and I was going to be part of some memorable moments. It took me 17 years, as I sit here in 2019 reading through the final updates to my book, to get all my thoughts together for the first of what I hope will be many books that I'll share with the world.

The one thing I realized, in taking these notes and keeping a lot of events, writing down everything that came to mind related to my life and my book, taking pictures and storing them for memories, was this: I truly believe the theory and suggestions from my chapter "Take Only the Good Pictures." It is amazing when I look back over the events that have taken place in my life, especially in the last 10 years, and realize all the great things I have experienced. It is so easy for us to forget many of the details of our experiences, and I will tell you from my own situation, it has been fulfilling to look back at the things I have accomplished, evaluate what went well, what did not go well, and things I could have done differently.

When I say, "Keep a Diary," I'm not suggesting that you have a daily post with "Dear Diary" in your salutation. You can do this if it makes you feel good, but this is not necessarily a rundown of every event that took place in your life from the time you woke up until the time you went to bed each day. Nor do I feel that you have to take a daily note, unless you feel compelled to do so. Instead, what I suggest is that you track important events, quotes, things you think of while in the shower or driving, and things you want to remember far into your life. Thanks to the rise of mobile devices and digital media, I track my thoughts and ideas all over the place. Whether it's online, or in the notes app on my phone, I try to keep track of things that are going on in my life.

When I started speaking at multiple events all over the world, I began to post on my blog site a list of each event I attended so I would not forget them. I am so glad I did this. Because I now am sitting here in 2019, looking at the events I was part of since 2012, and I know that the dates, locations, and activities of each of them would begin to blur as I took on more opportunities. I now have a way to look at each event, what I spoke for those events, and be proud as I see where I have come over the years.

For my book, between the years 2002 to 2019, I took note after note when I heard great things that I wanted to include in my book. Sometimes I would have an idea pop into my head for a new chapter, and I would quickly open my notes app and take it down. One thing I never expected was, as I have grown older, I have so many things going on around me with my work, my speaking, my person life, and my writings, that a great idea may pop into my head only for a moment, and if I'm not quick to take it down, I forget the topic when I try to recall it later. Writing it down saves the memory for later.

When you evaluate the pros and cons, it's always positive for taking notes and keeping a diary. Many chapter titles, many notes within this very book, were ideas I took while riding down the road, sitting in traffic, standing in the shower, or just sitting at my desk thinking. You would not have received my chapter on "Slower Traffic Keep Right," for example, if I did not take notes the moment an idea popped into my head.

Take notes on everything. My suggestion would be not to worry about the structure of the notes initially. Do not waste time worrying about whether you need to have sections or groups like "Work," "Home," "School," "Special Projects." It is fine if you decide to come up with groups to keep your notes in separate areas. My suggestion would be to throw them all together just to get started, and then hash them out into the groups when you go back and read them. You might be thinking that you are only going to write on one specific group or topic. That is fine as well. The key is to get started and take notes. Visit them often, add to them, and let the notes speak to you, motivate you, and allow yourself to become stronger, more dedicated, and successful in the process.

Track your life. Someday you will look back on all you have done and feel a strong sense of accomplishment. Most importantly, someday you can share these notes and ideas with your family and friends. Just another way to leave a legacy.

Chapter 29:
It's Your Two-Minute Warning

"Desperate times call for desperate measures."

Unknown

Anyone who is a fan of professional football knows, when there are two minutes left on the clock in the first half and second half, there is a "two-minute warning." Many years ago, this process began due to the lack of technology to ensure that the football stadium's clock matched the official time remaining in the game. The officiating crew of referees would use the short break when there were two minutes left on the clock to ensure that their clocks and the stadium clocks were in sync.[1]

Today we see the two-minute warning being used for the commentators to discuss how they think the game will proceed in those final two minutes of the half, their predictions for what they think each team will do, and their initial take on a summary of the half.

When teams return from the break, many call this the "two-minute drill" as teams begin to pull out their best game plans, their most strategic plays, and you see teams making decisions and plays that were not seen during the rest of the game.[2] Teams that are losing and behind will become more aggressive and drive to tie or win the game before time expires. Teams that are ahead and winning will typically play cautious and conservative to keep the lead and protect their win.

The team that is successful, regardless of the score at the two-minute warning, is the team that figures out the strategy that needs to be played to keep the lead or eliminate the deficit. The final two minutes become a mental game, a game of strategies and taking chances to preserve a win.

This same concept can be applied to many situations in our lives. And I see this in three different scenarios:

Scenario 1: The Procrastinator

So many times, we live day-to-day, working the day job, going to school, working at home, or planning our day by doing the same things, within a standard routine. We wait until the last minute to get focused, to ensure that we "win." We become extreme procrastinators and we put off things that we could do today to bring us success tomorrow and in the future. Reduce your tendency to procrastinate, give an extra effort today even when you don't feel like doing so. Do one thing each day that you didn't think you would do until later.

Scenario 2: The Winner

Some of you may be saying, "Mike, I'm not a procrastinator. I plan my tasks and goals and I achieve them every day." I'm proud of you. And I want to be just like you someday! But I'm sorry to say that there is more you can do in those times when you can go above and beyond the call. Many people take pride in setting goals and meeting them. They take pride in building their task list every morning or week, and checking things off one by one until they do everything they planned. It's been said that the difference between winning and losing is sometimes only inches. We see Olympians racing head to head in competition and then in the last seconds of the race, one steps a tenth of a second ahead and wins. To be the winner, sometimes you have to do even more than just be good. Sometimes you have to do more than just being the best or great at what you do. Sometimes you have to give the extra 10 percent above all you have — and that will set you apart from the others. Each day, when you are being your best and achieving all of your tasks and goals, ask yourself, "What more could I do? What can I do differently today to become even better in the future?"

Scenario 3: The Closer

We've heard of bucket lists. So many people have them. We build enormous dream lists, which contain things we have never done but want to do before our lives are over. It may be to accomplish some great tasks in your life. It may be to travel to some place you have never been. It may be to meet someone you have never met before. It may simply be to reach a role in your career or life that you never thought you could accomplish. Regardless, as you read this, I can assure you that you have time. Your two-minute warning may not be here yet, but you do not have to wait until it arrives to go for those bucket list goals. I'm here to tell you that we don't always know the time we have left in the game of life. We are not always guaranteed that next day, that next hour, or another year to reach where we want to be. Seize the opportunity while you have the strength, the health, the courage, and the time to do it. You don't have to wait until you are told that the "two-minute warning" of your life has arrived and you realize the clock is ticking down. Build your list, go for your goals, and ensure you leave this life with a list of things you hoped and planned to accomplish throughout.

Whatever your scenario, and wherever you are in the game, you must plan for your two-minute warning, and realize those times when you need to step up your game plan, redesign your strategy, and focus on everything you need to do in order to come out a winner.

Tick-tock, tick-tock, tick-tock . . . The clock is ticking . . .

Chapter 30:
Leave a Legacy

"It has been said that the two most important days
of a man's life are the day on which he was born and
the day on which he discovers why he was born."

Ernest T. Campbell, "Give Ye Them to Eat" (sermon)[1]

When I was seven years old, I attended a family wedding. On my return from that wedding, I sat down at the piano and began to play the wedding march song. Everyone was surprised. It became evident to my parents that I should be taking piano lessons. For the next nine years, I took lessons to build upon my musical ability. My love for music spanned beyond just the piano. I played in the band in school, I listened to every type of music the radio would play, and I played for each church I attended through the years.

Many times, the person you are, the things you like, and the talents you have are genetically passed down to your children. I was no exception to this rule. My two brilliant children were born with a love of music. Both play the piano, both sing music, both have won singing competitions, and both have a love for all types of music. I've said that my children are probably the youngest ones to know almost every '80s song that exists.

I tell you this story because I realize the happiness that comes with seeing your legacy right in front of you. I have been blessed to achieve many great things in my life. I have received honors in school and work. I have reached many of the goals that I set out to accomplish in my career and life. With each of these satisfying and fulfilling events, I have taken pride in my accomplishments. But anyone who has ever been a parent will tell you that no pride and fulfillment within yourself will ever compare to the pride of seeing your children achieve success and greatness.

Each of us is given a limited number of years in this life. How you choose to live that life is your choice. We waste so much time doing things that do not matter at all in the grand scheme of things. We spend our time watching television, hours and hours on social media, and lose significant opportunities to make a difference in the world and leave a legacy.

The world we live in is not making any of this easier. We've gone from telephones attached to the wall at home and computers on a desk somewhere, to a world where we carry a telephone, computer, internet browser, notepad, camera, and music player all on one handheld device in our pocket. Everything is moving at a faster pace now more than ever in the history of human life.

As I grow older, I'm reminded of the great people I have been blessed to spend my life with — especially my grandparents, aunts, uncles, cousins, friends, coworkers, and most importantly my parents. I'm reminded daily of the legacy that has been given to me to carry on, and all of the lessons I have learned in this life that I have been able to modify and improve as I share with my own children, friends, and relatives.

While there is a long list of all the things I strived to accomplish, I am constantly reminded that each and every thing I do in this life needs to feed my ultimate goal, and that is to leave a legacy. I want to be remembered for something. I want my legacy to be left in the minds of others long after I am gone.

Your legacy does not have to be the same as mine. In fact, you should strive to be different from all the others. The special skill that makes up your core values needs to be shared with the world. We were not born to just live and die. Each of us has a purpose. What is your legacy? What do you hope to accomplish in this life in such a way that others remember you? Is it a book? Is it a charity event or some type of volunteer work that you wish to support? Is it helping others in need? Is it a great new invention or product that the world will use for years to follow? Is it to help grow your current company or organization? Is it to start your *own* company? Or is it simply to provide a memory to your relatives, children, and grandchildren of your core values and purpose in this life?

We all have the potential to make a difference while we are alive. The best part is, each of us has the exact same amount of time each day to do that very thing. Zig Ziglar said, "We all have 24-hour days." What are you doing with each minute, each hour, each day of your life?

Before I wrap this chapter up, and ultimately this whole book, I want to share with you one thing that you may have already realized. If you haven't realized what I am about to tell you, I am confident you will before you reach the end of this journey. And that is, your goals, your dreams, your aspirations, and your legacy may change throughout your life. They may even change daily. This is absolutely okay. Keep refining and rebuilding your plan. Keep adjusting your view of what you are good at and what you can give to the world. Nothing is wrong with change. Find what you do best, and continue to do it better than anyone else.

This book was one of the major things I wanted to share with the world as part of my legacy. My book may never be on your list of "the best books I have ever read," but I do hope you enjoyed the journey with me. I hope and pray that at least one thing I said in this book gave you that tiny spark, which will ultimately become a fire that will burn within you and keep you on track to achieve greatness in this life.

Have you decided what your legacy will be in this life? If not, keep evaluating everything. It will find you.

Thank you for taking this short journey with me. If I can ever support you, give you clarity on your core values, or simply listen to your story, you know how to reach me.

About the Author

Mike W. Lyles is an international speaker, author, IT professional, mentor, and coach in North Carolina. Mike is a graduate of Appalachian State University with a degree in computer science. He began his work as a software engineer, writing software programs for various companies. He then became a team lead, and eventually a manager for multiple teams. Mike realized his love and passion for leading, guiding, coaching, and mentoring others very early. For over 25 years, Mike has led hundreds of team members, driving the successful delivery of major programs.

Mike realized that while contributing to an organization can bring much success, his passion was focused on being a coach and mentor, driving teams to grow, and motivating new leaders within the organizations where he has worked. Through many years, Mike has focused his work on motivating the key contributors to each team, as well as coaching the leads and managers on his team to grow in their careers as well.

Through a very long career in IT, Mike realized that lessons in leadership and success can be taken from both good and bad leaders. He has developed successful programs that capitalize on both the good and the bad things taken from over two decades of corporate career experiences.

Mike began writing technical documents for multiple publications in 2011 and began speaking at multiple conferences and events in 2012. Since then, Mike has shared his experiences across five continents and multiple countries. Mike has been a member of Toastmasters International, where he served as the president of his local club in 2016.

Mike is inspired by helping others to grow in their career and personal growth. He has mentored and coached many people through the years, and is working on his next book, which will be focused on leadership within various organizations and teams.

To know more about Mike, follow him on social media, and connect with him, please view the following sites:

Websites:	www.MikeWLyles.com
	www.TheDriveThruBook.com
Twitter	@MikeLyles
Facebook	https://www.facebook.com/mikelylesbusiness/
LinkedIn	https://www.linkedin.com/in/mikewlyles
Instagram	@MikeLyles
YouTube	http://www.youtube.com/user/mikewlyles

Stay tuned. This will not be the last book you see from Mike Lyles!

Notes

Chapter 6 – My Mom and Steve Jobs

1. Steve Jobs, "2005 Stanford Commencement Address," filmed June 12, 2005 at Stanford University, video, 15:04, https://www.youtube.com / watch?v=UF8uR6Z6KLc.

2. "'You've Got to Find What You Love,' Steve Jobs Says," Commencement Address, Stanford University, June 14, 2005, https:// news.stanford.edu /news/2005/june15/jobs-061505.html.

3. "Ask the Tester: Mike Lyles," Software Test Professionals, March 9, 2012, https://www.softwaretestpro.com/ask-the-tester-mike-lyles/.

Chapter 8 – Who Will Win the Super Bowl

1. "Team History," Pittsburgh Steelers, Pro Football Hall of Fame, accessed September 1, 2019, https://www.profootballhof.com/teams/ pittsburgh-steelers/team-history/.

2. Jason Duaine Hahn, "These Five Friends Have Attended Every Single Super Bowl Together," People, February 2, 2018, https://people.com/ sports /super-bowl-2018-five-friends-attended-every-game/.

Chapter 16 – Time Does Not Equal Money

1. Benjamin Franklin, "Advice to a Young Tradesman," Founders Online, National Archives, accessed September 1, 2019, https:// founders.archives.gov/documents/Franklin/01-03-02-0130.

Chapter 20 – Don't Die before You're Dead

1. "JK Rowling Portrait," National Treasures, *The Telegraph*, June 26, 2008, https://www.telegraph.co.uk/news/newstopics/nationaltreasures /2193390/JK-Rowling-portrait.html.

2. Steven Loeb, "When WhatsApp Was Young: The Early Years," Vator News, August 1, 2017, https://vator.tv/ news/2017-08-01-when-whatsapp-was-young-the-early-years.

3. "Henry Ford," History.com, updated June 6, 2019, https://www. history .com/topics/inventions/henry-ford.

4. "The Chronicle of Coco-Cola: The Candler Era," History, The Coca-Cola Company, January 1, 2012, https://www.coca-colacompany.com /stories/the-chronicle-of-coca-cola-the-candler-era.

5. "Famous Japanese People: Soichiro Honda," Japanese Visitor, accessed September 1, 2019, https://www.japanvisitor.com/japanese-culture/famous -japanese/soichiro-honda.

6. "Sam Walton," Our History, Walmart, accessed September 1, 2019, https://corporate.walmart.com/our-story/our-history.

7. "Thomas Edison & the History of Electricity," General Electric, accessed September 1, 2019, https://www.ge.com/about-us/history/ thomas-edison.

8. "These Eight Startup Founders Prove You Don't Have to Be Young to Win in Tech," CNBC, July 4, 2018, https://www.cnbc. com/2018/06/28/tech-founders-45.html.

9. "Gordon Bowker, 51 — Entrepreneur, Founder of Starbucks," The 50 Plus Achievers Club, accessed September 1, 2019, http://50plusachievers.club /inspiration/achievers/ item/76-gordon-bowker-51-entrepreneur-founder-of-starbucks.

10. "Our History," McDonalds, accessed September 1, 2019, https://www .mcdonalds.com/us/en-us/about-us/our-history.html.

11. "These Eight Startup Founders Prove You Don't Have to Be Young to Win in Tech," CNBC, July 4, 2018, https://www.cnbc. com/2018/06/28/tech-founders-45.html.

12. "A.P. Giannini," *Encyclopedia Britannica*, accessed September 1, 2019, https://www.britannica.com/biography/A-P-Giannini.

13. "Charles Ranlett Flint, 61 — Entrepreneur, Founder of IBM," The 50 Plus Achievers Club, accessed September 1, 2019, http://50plusachievers.club /inspiration/achievers/ item/77-charles-ranlett-flint-61-entrepreneur-founder-of-ibm.

14. Richard Feloni, "KFC Founder Colonel Sanders Didn't Achieve His Remarkable Success until His 60s," *Business Insider*, June 25, 2015, https://www.businessinsider.com/how-kfc-founder-colonel-sanders-achieved-success-in-his-60s-2015-6.

15. "Did You Know the World's Oldest Runner Is an Indian? Meet the Turbaned Tornado Fauja Singh!" The Better India, July 15, 2015, https://www .thebetterindia.com/23273/ story-of-fauja-singh-worlds-oldest-marathon-runner/.

Chapter 22 – Are You Comparing or Competing?

1. Jesse Yomtov, "Full List of Every Olympic Medal Michael Phelps Has Won," *USA Today*, updated August 14, 2016, https://www.usatoday .com/story/sports/olympics/rio-2016/2016/08/07/michael-phelps-medals /88361712/.

2. "Chad le Clos Snatches Gold from Phelps in 200m Butterfly Final Drama," Olympic.org, accessed September 1, 2019, https://www. olympic.org /videos/chad-le-clos-snatches-gold-from-phelps-in-200m-butterfly-final-drama.

3. "Michael Phelps Exits the Olympics, and Enters Retirement at 27," NPR, posted August 12, 2012, https://www.npr.org/sections/thetorch/2012/08 /08/158422864/michael-phelps-exits-the-olympics-and-enters-retirement-at-27.

4. "Rio 2016: Michael Phelps' Last Challenge," Olympic.org, posted March 11, 2016, https://www.olympic.org /news/rio-2016-michael-phelps-last-challenge.

5. Ashley Hoffman, "Michael Phelps Explains What Was Really Going on With His Iconic Phelps Game Face," *Time*, August 16, 2016, https://time .com/4455032/rio-2016-olympics-michael-phelps-face-2/.

6. Cady Lang, "A Guide to Why the Internet Is Losing It Over Michael Phelps Beating Chad le Clos," *Time*, August 10, 2016, https://time.com /4446837/rio-2016-olympics-michael-phelps-chad-le-clos/.

Chapter 23 – Who Needs a Leader?

1. Liz Wizeman, "How the Best Leaders Make Everyone Smarter," interview by Dorie Clark, *Forbes*, November 26, 2013, https://www.forbes.com/sites /dorieclark/2013/11/26/how-the-best-leaders-make-everyone-smarter/.

2. Aimee Groth, "Zappos Is Struggling with Holocracy Because Humans Aren't Designed to Operate Like Software," *Quartz*, December 21, 2016, https://qz.com/849980/zappos-is-struggling-with-holacracy-because-humans-arent-designed-to-operate-like-software/.

3. Tony Hsieh, "For Zappos' Tony Hsieh, 'Holocracy' Is the Right Fit," interview by Adam Grant, The Wharton School of the University of Pennsylvania, https://knowledge.wharton .upenn.edu/article/zappos-tony-hsieh-holocracy-right-fit/.

4. Lauren French, "Zappos' Weird Management Style Is Costing It More Employees," *Time*, January 14, 2016, https://time.com/4180791/zappos-holacracy-buyouts/.

Chapter 26 – The Fastest Car Doesn't Always Win the Race

1. "How Prohibition Gave Birth to NASCAR," History.com, updated August 29, 2018, https://www.history.com/news/how-prohibition-gave-birth-to-nascar.

2. "Pit stop," Wikipedia, accessed September 1, 2019, https://en.wikipedia .org/wiki/Pit_stop.

3. Christopher Olmstead, "NASCAR: Ranking the 10 Biggest Fights in NASCAR History," Fox Sports, June 30, 2017, https://www.foxsports. com/nascar/story/nascar-ranking-the-10-biggest-fights-in-nascar-history-012017.

Chapter 29 – It's Your Two-Minute Warning

1. "Two-minute warning," Wikipedia, accessed September 1, 2019, https://en.wikipedia.org /wiki/Two-minute_warning.

2. "NFL 101: Introducing the Basics of the Two-Minute Offense," Bleacher Report, June 27, 2015, https://bleacherreport.com/articles /2504050-nfl-101-introducing-the-basics-of-the-two-minute-offense; "Hurry-up offense," Wikipedia, accessed September 1, 2019, https:// en.wikipedia.org /wiki/Hurry-up_offense.

Chapter 30 – Leave a Legacy

1. Ernest T. Campbell, "Sermon: Give ye them to eat," Archive.org, accessed September 1, 2019, https://archive.org/stream/sermon-giveyethem00camp /sermongiveyethem00camp_djvu.txt. Note: This quote has been attributed to many others as noted in this

blog post: Matt Seybold, "The Apocryphal Twain: 'The Two Most Important Days of Your Life . . .'" The Center for Mark Twain Studies (blog), December 6, 2016, https://marktwain studies.com/the-apocryphal-twain-the-two-most-important-days-of-your-life/.

References

Brown, Brené. *The Gifts of Imperfection.* Center City, MN: Hazelden, 2010.

Collins, Jim. *Good to Great.* New York: HarperCollins, 2001.

Cooper, Robert. *The Other 90%.* New York: Crown Business, 2002.

Covey, Stephen R. *The 7 Habits of Highly Effective People.* New York: Simon & Schuster, 1989

———. *The 8th Habit.* New York: Free Press, 2004.

———. *First Things First: To Live, to Love, to Learn, to Leave a Legacy.* New York: Fireside, 1995.

Fox, Jeffrey J. *How to Become CEO.* New York: Hyperion, 1998.

Frankl, Viktor E. *Man's Search for Meaning.* Boston: Beacon Press, 2006.

Sinek, Simon. *Start with Why.* New York: Penguin Group, 2009.

Warren, Rick. *The Purpose Driven Life.* Grand Rapids, MI: Zondervan, 2002.

Wiseman, Liz. *Multipliers.* New York: Harper Business, 2017.

Ziglar, Zig. *Secrets of Closing the Sale.* Grand Rapids, MI: Fleming H. Revell, 1984.